REACHING PAST THE WIRE

Curt – Thank you for your support of this project.
Deanna

REACHING PAST THE WIRE

A Nurse at Abu Ghraib

LIEUTENANT COLONEL
Deanna Germain
USAR (Retired)

with
Connie Lounsbury

**BOREALIS
BOOKS**

Borealis Books is an imprint of the Minnesota Historical Society Press.

www.borealisbooks.org

Most of the names used in this book have been changed.

The quotation on page 209 is from "Nursing in the Shadow of Abu Ghraib," part of *Inside Iraq,* a series of articles by Janet Boivin published in *Nursing Spectrum* magazine in 2005 (available at http://www.nursingspectrum.com/iraq/).

Photographs on pages 90 (bottom), 100 (bottom), and 101 (both) were provided by Specialist Gray of the 67th CSH, Würzberg, Germany.

The Minnesota Historical Society Press is a member of the Association of American University Presses.

Manufactured in the United States of America

10 9 8 7 6 5 4 3 2 1

⊗ The paper used in this publication meets the minimum requirements of the American National Standard for Information Sciences—Permanence for Printed Library Materials, ANSI Z39.48–1984.

International Standard Book Number
ISBN 13: 978-0-87351-606-8
ISBN 10: 0-87351-606-0

Library of Congress
Cataloging-in-Publication Data

Germain, Deanna, 1950–
Reaching past the wire : a nurse at Abu Ghraib / Deanna Germain, with Connie Lounsbury.
    p.   cm.
ISBN-13: 978-0-87351-606-8
  (cloth : alk. paper)
ISBN-10: 0-87351-606-0
  (cloth : alk. paper)
  1. Germain, Deanna, 1950–
  2. Iraq War, 2003—Personal
    narratives, American.
  3. Nurse practitioners—Iraq—
    Biography.
  4. Abu Ghraib Prison.
  5. Iraq War, 2003—Prisoners and
    prisons, American.
  I. Lounsbury, Connie, 1941–
  II. Title.
DS79.76.G474 2007
956.7044'37—dc22
2007017313

For my family

REACHING PAST THE WIRE

Preface

I LOOK BACK, AND IT SEEMS SURREAL. On some days, it feels like it happened yesterday. On other days, it plays back like someone else's story.

I was a fifty-two-year-old wife, mother, grandmother, nurse practitioner, and Army Reserve lieutenant colonel living the American dream in Minnesota. I went from comfortable middle-class suburbia to sleeping in Saddam Hussein's old prison at Abu Ghraib, caring for Iraqi prisoners and praying every day to stay alive. Yet I would do it all again.

I am frequently asked what it was like to be at Abu Ghraib. How can I answer that, chatting in the aisle of the grocery store?

"I was shot at a lot"?

"I slept in a cement cell with no electricity where the temperature was usually over a hundred degrees"?

"The supply lines were so bad that we had to make colostomy bags out of plastic bags"?

I trained a lifetime for the possibility of using skills that

I was called upon to use in Iraq. But I never expected to be changed by—and to change—the lives of so many people I met along this journey. Truly, it is God's plan that not one of us is insignificant in this life.

The soldiers and civilians I cared for at Abu Ghraib, the Sunni, Kurdish, Shia, and Christian Iraqi translators who became friends, the civilian contractors from many countries, and my fellow soldiers working in the hospital—all taught me about myself and about a world I had not imagined. My life, which was threatened every day I served at Abu Ghraib, is richer now because of the people I met there.

This is not a chronicle about war or the military. You can look to the daily newspapers and other media for that. I write about my daily life and that of the soldiers and Marines I served with at the military hospital at Abu Ghraib Prison; how health care is administered during wartime; the civilians who work alongside the soldiers; the lives of many innocent and not-so-innocent Iraqis with whom I came into contact every day. This book is about the place, the people, and me.

It is my hope that this book will change the way you see the place and the people and, perhaps, even your own heart.

REACHING PAST THE WIRE

Six Days to Ready

I answered the door and saw the certified letter from the United States Army Reserve. Activation orders—DAMN! The waiting and wondering were over.

As I signed a receipt for the letter held out to me that frigid February afternoon in 2003, I knew I was signing for a life-changing event. I also knew that others in my Army Reserve unit were going through the same thing— probably at the same time.

This wasn't really a surprise. With things heating up in Iraq, and with my unit being a combat support hospital unit that could be sent overseas, I had been expecting we might be deployed. Worsening news reports had added to my apprehension, as did frequent questions from friends and family: "Have you heard anything yet? Are you going to be deployed?" I had started to feel like I was in limbo. "Finally we know," I thought, walking slowly back to the kitchen with the letter.

I sat in a chair and Dave, my husband, came in, asking, "Who was that?" Then, seeing the certified letter in my hand, just like the one that mobilized me to active duty during Desert Storm in 1991, his eyes took on the "I know what that is" look. I slit open the envelope and began silently reading:

> *Lieutenant Colonel Deanna Germain:*
>
> *You are ordered to Active Duty as a member of your Reserve Component unit for the period indicated unless sooner released or unless extended. Proceed from your current location in sufficient time to report by the date specified. You enter active duty upon reporting to unit home station.*
>
> *Report to: 801st Combat Support Hospital, Ft. Sheridan, Illinois on 1 March 2003.*
>
> *Report to Fort Stewart Georgia on 1 March 2003.*
>
> *Period of active duty: 365 days*
>
> *Purpose of mobilization: For Enduring Freedom*

The notice included more addresses and abbreviations, but I looked at the calendar on the wall. "I leave in six days!" I said. "Six days!" I handed Dave the letter.

My stoic military brain kicked in immediately, and I grabbed a pad of paper to make a list of things I needed to do. Dave read the letter and then looked at me, reality setting in.

"I'll miss six months of Yasmine's life," I said as I looked for a pen. History assured me that Reserve units are not kept active for more than six months at a time. My beautiful little granddaughter was only nine months old. Our daughter Laura and her husband live close by, and I saw YaYa often. I began, already, to mourn the "firsts" that I would miss in YaYa's life—her first steps, her first words, her first birthday.

My thoughts next moved to the possibility of imminent war in Iraq. The official U.S. position was that Iraq illegally possessed weapons of mass destruction in violation of United Nations Security Council Resolution 1441, and we were working to disarm them through diplomatic means. UN inspection teams had already been searching Iraq for the alleged weapons for nearly three months.

Everyone in our unit knew the possibility of being activated at any time, yet the reality of it—and the immediacy of it—sent me into a momentary panic. Would this escalate into a full-scale war? We were in a high-tempo period with much troop movement. Would I be sent into a war zone? Would I be killed or injured? I tried to focus on my to-do list, but I was having trouble regulating my breath.

I felt numb, sad, and dizzy, all at the same time. What to do first? What next?

I had told my soldiers, "Be prepared; get your things packed, and put your important papers where you can get your hands on them quickly." This would be their first activation. I had been through it before, but I knew this deployment was going to be different.

I began making a list—backward planning, as I had always done. What did I have to do on each of the next six days, from the last to the first, to be prepared to leave home, family, work, church, and community for six months?

I had to button down things at the pain clinic where I work as a nurse practitioner. Turn my patient files over to others. Say good-bye to my family, friends, neighbors.

Don't forget the Casablanca coffee shop workers, who sold me a latte nearly every day. Give proxies to others for my responsibilities as college alumni treasurer and assorted committee positions. Under different circumstances, I would have felt like I was dumping on others, but now I had no choice—no time for guilt.

I did this before; I can do it again, I told myself over and over as I moved down my list of tasks, fighting against time. Packing. Phone calls. Paperwork. Hurry. Hurry. Sometimes I had to stop myself, reorganize my thoughts, stay on track.

The phone calls started coming and didn't stop. "No, I don't know where we're going." "No, I don't know how long I'll be gone." Anxiety from friends and family members increased my tension. "Don't worry. I'll be okay." My parents, who had raised me on a dairy farm near Fairfax, Minnesota, had been through this twelve years earlier, when my brother-in-law and I were both called up for the Gulf War—but that didn't make it easier on them. I had served stateside then, and now my mother couldn't understand why the military would send someone of my age into a war zone at the end of my military career. My quiet, reserved father, who had served in the military, was concerned for my safety, but he knew I was doing what I had to do.

The Army Reserve just works that way: we go when we're called. Most Reservists enlist into, serve in, and retire from the USAR. (Officers, who agree to serve for a number of years, can be called back.) Soldiers in the active army have an option to finish out their contracts in the Reserves; if they're then called up for duty, they remain Reservists. Like people in the National Guard, we have civilian jobs and perform training or service once a month—but Guard units report to the Department of Defense through their state's governor and are typically mobilized as entire units. We report through regional readiness commands, and we can be mobilized either individually or in our units.

I packed my military gear—uniforms, boots, vest pouches that carry ammunition, poncho, mat for my cot—in the standard way. A strange mix of dread and excitement stirred around me. I always remembered one more thing I had to do before I sat down, and I never sat down. During rare quiet moments, I asked myself, *Am I really ready to do the job I'll be expected to do?* The old army motto, "Be All That You Can Be," reverberated in my head. *How good can I be, and will it be good enough?*

I went to the drugstore to pick up some toothpaste, and everyone else in the store acted as if it was life as usual. Well, it wasn't life as usual for me. I felt frenzied. I felt hollow. I was afraid. The lines were long. Everyone seemed to be moving in slow motion. I wanted to say, "Can't you hurry? I'm leaving. I don't know when I'm coming back. I can't be sure I *am* coming back. Don't you understand?"

I found myself looking at Dave more—studying his face. I wanted to remember every feature. We updated our wills. I felt the weight of the world on my shoulders.

Baby Yasmine looked at me as I told her things she couldn't understand but that I needed to say. I wanted to remember the silk in her cheeks and the sunshine in her giggle, and I needed to hold my family close and make sure they knew how much they meant to me. At times, no words would come at all, and I could only say a silent prayer of thanks for these, my precious blessings.

The simplest of things took on a special meaning— a time of "lasts." *Won't be doing this again before I leave,* I chuckled to myself as I did laundry, took out the garbage, and vacuumed the living room.

As the departure date approached, I began distancing myself from my family. I spent more time with my military friends, talking on the phone with them a great deal and making hurried trips to Fort Snelling to say good-bye to those who were leaving before me. We were all speculating as to where we would be going and how it would be. The same drama, with variation, was happening to everyone in our unit. Packing our gear, deciding who's going to pay the bills while we're gone, who's going to do the lawn work, who's going to take the baby. Like everyone else, I acted as if I was okay—ready to do this.

Those of us from Minnesota had been told to report to our home station, Fort Snelling, on March 1. The evening before my departure our family went to dinner at Maca- roni Grill. The event was a rite of passage—finalizing the family good-bye. It felt like a formal moment as we went through the motions, trying to be upbeat and happy. I had trouble swallowing my food. Laura was quiet, wiping away tears when she thought I wasn't looking, her smile forced. I had loved my daughter's face from the day she was born, yet now I was trying to memorize every feature, just as I had done with the snowy landscape of our Minnesota community on the drive to the restaurant. I filed away into my memory bank the sharp sting of inhaled frigid air. The white linen napkin felt smooth in my lap, and I wondered when I would again eat in a nice restaurant.

Sounds of other diners' laughter surrounded us, but the only one not trying to force gaiety at our table was YaYa, who was her usual bubbly self, eating bits of food with her fingers. By the time we left the restaurant, I was glad to stop trying to act as if nothing was changing.

The next morning Dave drove me the forty-minute trip to Fort Snelling. We stopped at Laura's for another hug, and we took a couple of pictures together with me in my uniform. Of course we felt very sad, and we all had tears, but we tried to be stoic.

As soon as we left Laura's, the getting ready was over. I was in military mode. My mind was mostly on whether I had forgotten anything. When I left Dave, I didn't know if I would be staying at Fort Snelling and able to see him again soon or if we would be going directly to Chicago.

Dave was supportive of my doing my duty as a Reserve soldier, and I became increasingly grateful for that. He was extremely sad to see me leave, and sent me off with bravado that neither of us felt but both needed to pretend. I took what comfort I could in the knowledge that his friends and his colleagues at the public works department would be supportive while I was away. I also knew that as an avid outdoorsman he would find plenty to occupy his time on the weekends with his friends.

Those of us reassigned from the 114th Combat Support Hospital (csH) Unit to the 801st csH Unit in Chicago were flown from Fort Snelling to Chicago that day. The other half of the 114th was reassigned elsewhere and, with few exceptions, never did leave the States. Several days later, our newly reconstituted group, about five hundred soldiers, was sent to Fort Stewart, Georgia, home of the Third Infantry Division.

There we received physical training, weapons training, combat training, convoy training, and gas mask training. We set up a DepMeds (Deployable Medical System) hospital, which is a standard army tent mobile field hospital with operating rooms, X-ray suites, and wards, all outfitted with climate controls and current medical equipment. We had mock hospital care training and updated our CPR and medical expertise.

We also faced an underlying challenge in this newly reconstituted unit: we were bringing people together from multiple units who had never worked with each other. The commander and his staff had to decide how to position people to make a good, strong unit. Then the personnel had to adjust to new leadership and new styles in order to work effectively together.

We were told to select battle buddies, an informal pairing through which you were accountable for each other at all times. Lieutenant Colonel Cheryl Proper and I became battle buddies and close friends. She was also new to the 801st, reassigned from the 337th CSH from Indiana, and we teased each other about everything from our accents to our football teams. I insisted I didn't have an accent. Of course, everyone had seen the movie *Fargo*, and they said I sounded just like the movie. The more I denied it, the more they laughed at my "accented" words of denial.

Officers and enlisted personnel all trained together with the same requirements. The only separate instruction I had was in weapons training, as officers carry 9-millimeter handguns as opposed to the M16 rifles enlisted soldiers carry. Life became hell for us if we failed to run far enough, hit the target the required number of times, or put our gas masks on in nine seconds. We needed to be able to take care of ourselves, and others around us, in a combat situation. Our training reminded us that war is a life-or-death proposition, and we were looking at going to war. We were training for the real deal.

All of us struggled to get used to being away from our loved ones. I kept in touch with most of my family and friends by e-mail and called Dave often, as that is how we preferred to communicate. He and Laura were coping, but Laura was having a difficult time. I was grateful they were close to each other.

During that uncertain time, the UN searched for weapons of mass destruction in Iraq with the imminent invasion of the country at hand. A lot of rumors circulated as to what, if anything, our role was going to be in this war. We were even told at one time that we were going home. I sent my boots back to Minnesota.

On March 19, 2003, President George W. Bush, in a coalition with forces of the United Kingdom, Australia, and Poland, ordered U.S. military forces to launch an invasion of Iraq, beginning the war. The Iraqi military was quickly defeated, and Baghdad fell on April 9. This ended the regime of Saddam Hussein and toppled the Ba'ath Party.

Looting and riots were unleashed in Baghdad. As the violence increased, so did our anxiety. The big question for us at Fort Stewart was what were we training for: Where would we end up? When? Would we be sent somewhere dangerous? We were living with, and training hard for, the big "If."

We didn't have to wait too long. At the end of April, two months after deployment, 120 of us got orders for Kuwait. Camp Wolf, a huge tent city near the Kuwait City Airport, would be our first home. We would take over an ongoing mission at the Kuwait Armed Forces Hospital from the 865th CSH from New York. The commander appointed me chief nurse for this mission.

This was it. Dave sent back my boots. We were headed to the combat zone.

120 Degrees and Rising

A combination of excitement and fear, multiplied by one hundred and twenty of us, saturated the atmosphere as we boarded a Delta airplane for the trip from Fort Stewart to Kuwait. It was the most emotionally charged moment in my career thus far. There we were, all in our desert uniforms, weapons by our side, ready to do our duty for our country. We all knew we were embarking on a life-changing experience.

The airline staff treated us like heroes. They served us wonderful food and did everything they could to make us comfortable. When we landed in Rome to refuel, although we were not allowed to set foot on Italian soil, we stood on the steps and waved to people who were waving at us. We breathed in the air of Italy. Then we were back on our way.

Several hours later, the pilot welcomed us to Kuwait. "The temperature in Kuwait City is 120 degrees Fahrenheit," he announced.

I stepped out the door of the plane and felt like I had been hit in the face with the force of a giant hair dryer. The heat was overwhelming, and I sincerely wondered whether I would be able to survive six months of it. This was not just hot—this was damn hot! I was already sweating as I struggled to follow shouted orders: "Get your gear, get your water bottles, keep your water bottles with you at all times." *Welcome to Kuwait,* I thought wryly.

The Kuwait Armed Forces Hospital (KAFH) is in Kuwait City, about thirty minutes from Camp Wolf. As chief nurse I led the hospital nursing and support staff; I served on the team that managed the day-to-day operation of the hospital and the outpatient clinic at Camp Doha; and I coordinated the care for soldiers at outlying camps when needed. We provided services and medical care for all soldiers, Marines, coalition forces, and Department of Defense and contract civilians in Kuwait. With forty-five beds, we had sixty to seventy medical personnel working at the hospital in twelve-hour shifts. The other personnel in our unit were assigned to the various camps or other related areas.

We did not usually provide medical care for patients injured in direct combat, although, at least initially, we did get trauma patients from Baghdad and surrounding areas. Soldiers injured badly in Iraq came through Kuwait on their way to hospitalization in Landstuhl, Germany. As is the case in any hospital, we were either quiet or swamped with patients. We worked hard and saved a lot of lives during those many months.

Because Camp Wolf was located off the runways of Kuwait City Airport, we had jets flying overhead 24/7. The large, wood-floored tents had air conditioning and heaters, powered by generators, that worked some of the time; each held about twenty cots. We had shower trailers and the best large chow hall in Kuwait. On one of my days off, I even took a field trip across the border into Iraq, accompanying a friend who had to check bills of lading for a ship arriving at Umm Qasr.

Almost every soldier and Marine who transferred in and out of this theater of war passed through Camp Wolf, waiting for flights out of Kuwait or Iraq, buying souvenirs to bring or send home. We had a recreation hall with televisions, a game room, an outdoor basketball court, a small PX, and a few shops that sold trinkets. It was hot, dusty, and dirty, and we walked around the camp wearing our Physical Training (PT) uniforms—black shorts and gray T-shirts, both emblazoned with "Army"—trying to survive the heat.

We could always tell which soldiers and Marines came from Iraq without looking at their patches, just seeing them standing in line for food. Their uniforms had spots worn almost completely through. They looked disheveled and acted impatient. Their language was crude. They seemed hard-hearted—their attitude about everything was hard and rough. We could see in their faces and their actions that they were far away from what they were used to.

In August 2003, after I had been deployed for almost six months and in Kuwait for more than four months, Commander Henry Gilles and I attended a conference in Kuwait and met with planners at the brigade level. One of the logistics soldiers got up and said, "There are not enough medical personnel to rotate another group to the theater." She did not say, directly and specifically, that we would be in Kuwait longer than the expected six months,

but I read between the lines and I sure thought that was
what she was saying.

On the way back to camp the commander seemed un-
usually quiet. I said, "Sir, did I hear what I thought I heard?"

"Yes," Commander Gilles said with a sigh. "It's just a
matter of time until we get the orders. We won't tell the
troops until then."

My first reaction was sharp disappointment that we
wouldn't be home for Christmas. Yet my biggest concern
was for the soldiers in our unit. We all had built plans in
our minds about going back home, back to work. The
mental, emotional, financial, and personal toll of being
away so long could shake a person's very foundation, perhaps damaging our whole unit. Some soldiers were like little time bombs. How would they react to an extension?

The other great difficulty for me was in not being able
to share the news with anyone, not even Cheryl, who was
my head nurse at KAFH. But we in the Army knew that
the truth can—and does—change. No plan was final until it was enacted. Perhaps they would find replacements
for us after all. Yet I was quite confident that we would
be extended.

At the end of September 2003, when our soldiers were
wondering exactly when we would be sent home, Commander Gilles asked us all to be present at the hospital at
1830 hours. While we stood in the hallway, the commander announced that there were no replacements for
us as planned. He said, "We have been given notice that we
will be staying at the KAFH at least until January 2004." He
looked at us. "Any questions?" The whole unit was silent.
Reservists had never been mobilized for more than six

months. We had already been away from home for nearly seven months. The rules were obviously changing.

There went my tiny glimmer of hope that we wouldn't be extended. My disappointment was overshadowed by my concern for the other soldiers. I looked around to see how they were all taking the news.

A young female doctor let her tears flow down her face without trying to wipe them away. She had been eager to go home to her baby, who had been only a few months old when she left. My heart ached for her. A couple of soldiers just turned and walked away from the group without a word. No one tried to stop them. Others stood as if in shock.

After several stunned moments, someone said in a lighthearted voice, "Well, since we're going to be here for Thanksgiving and Christmas, let's get a committee together to make plans." That broke the spell. It then became a long night of phone calls home for all of us.

About a month later, our unit was moved to Camp Doha, thirty minutes away. Camp Doha was like a little city that housed thousands of soldiers. We lived in big hangars, like huge pole barns, with thousands of bunk beds. Our unit was placed together. Women were partitioned off, but anyone could look over the partition from a top bunk. Later, some of the command staff were moved to trailers nearby. Cheryl and I shared a trailer.

This military camp had a large PX, a big chow hall, a movie theater, a recreation center, a gym, souvenir shops, and many places to eat. Among them were KFC, Subway, Hardee's, Baskin-Robbins, and a pizza place.

When we moved to Camp Doha, a Starbucks came to camp. I was ecstatic, and I quickly became a regular. My two favorite baristas, Atik and Eduardo, cared about doing a good job for the soldiers and became special friends.

The holidays passed, and we eagerly awaited the coming of January 2004, but when January arrived, no one came to replace us. We were extended once again.

I had to make yet another difficult phone call to Dave. "I'm so sorry. We're still not going to be able to come home."

"What? You're not coming home?"

"Not now."

"Why? What happened?"

"They don't have replacements to take over the hospital."

"Oh, DeeDee, we were all expecting you home soon."

"I know. Me too."

"Are you doing okay?"

"You know me. I'll be okay. What choice do I have? It's just hard because I never expected to be here this long. How are you doing?"

"I'm fine. It's quiet. It's lonely here. But don't worry about me. Just get home as soon as you can."

"How's everyone else?"

"Everyone's fine. People keep calling. What should I tell them now?"

"Just say I'll be home as soon as I can. Anything else going on?"

"I had to replace the refrigerator. It just quit working. I bought pretty much the same thing we had before. That's about all."

"Okay. Well, I'll call you later. Hold off telling Laura until I have more information. I love you."

"I love you, too, DeeDee. Be safe."

I closed my cell phone but continued to sit in the quiet corner of the recreation center to savor the voice and the information a little longer. It had been a comfort to hear the mundane day-to-day things that were so unimportant to those at home but so very important to hear from so far away. *When would we be able to go home?*

In February, we finally learned that an active-duty Naval hospital unit would come in as replacements in mid-March. We did a hospital turnover at the end of March and began preparing to go home in early April 2004. We had done many things that touched the lives of soldiers in Kuwait. We were leaving with pride in a job well done.

We sent our books, boots, and extra gear home, knowing we would no longer need them. We completed our Army Physical Fitness Test, our evaluations, and all the other things that units do at the end of their mission. Everything was handed over. All the paperwork was done. We did our Post-Deployment Health Assessment Physical, the last thing on our "get out of Kuwait" list.

We called our families and told them we were coming home on April 10. April would be a great time to be back in Minnesota, with spring flowers and fresh green landscapes. I planned to take some time off before going back to work. Dave and I had talked about buying a lake home. It would be wonderful to be home for summer, relaxing with Dave at the shore of sparkling blue water, a cool breeze caressing my face. Long, lazy days to get reacquainted with YaYa. Time to catch up on Laura's life. The sweetness of anticipated pleasure put a perpetual smile on my hot, sweaty face.

Finally, we were going to leave from Camp Doha. On April 10, 2004, we had vacated our housing, our bags were on their way to the airport, and we had tickets for our freedom flight out of Kuwait. Only a certain number of soldiers could leave at a time because airplane space was so limited. We needed, and got, our tail numbers, the stamps that confirmed we were really leaving the theater of war.

We had final formation at 0700 hours. "Bring your bags to the truck at 0900 hours," said Commander Gilles. "That truck will bring your bags to customs, where you will collect your bags before final boarding. Your plane will depart at approximately 1600 hours." That gave us about two hours to get our bags on the truck and say our last good-byes. After loading my bags, I went to Starbucks at Camp Doha to keep my caffeine level up and bid farewell to my friends.

I was taking pictures with Atik and others when Cheryl came rushing around the corner. Her face was ashen, and the words tumbled out of her mouth: "We're not going anywhere."

"What do you mean?" I said.

"I don't know," Cheryl said, talking quickly, as she always did. "I just heard that we have to go back into formation as soon as possible and we're not leaving today."

"What?" I was stunned. I didn't think I heard her correctly. I didn't want to hear what she said. I pretended I hadn't. *Dave and Laura are expecting me to come home.* This was too unfair. It just wouldn't register as being true.

Cheryl was telling us that someone in headquarters had said something and it had spread like wildfire. "What does that mean, Madam?" Atik asked, his eyes huge and puzzled. "Will you be okay, Madam?"

I looked at my friends and said, "I don't know what's happening."

Back at formation, Commander Gilles seemed as surprised as the rest of us. "The Department of Defense has just announced that twenty thousand soldiers are being extended for a minimum of 120 days. We are among the twenty thousand. We are not going home."

Some of those twenty thousand soldiers were already in the planes on the tarmac at the time of the announcement. They had to disembark. Other planes already had wheels up on the way to Germany. Those soldiers were recalled back to the theater. Fifty-five Reserve units were affected that day, in addition to the many active-duty soldiers who were extended.

That day was the lowest point in this military deployment for me. Another extension! We had already served twice as long as we expected. It was so unfair!

Everyone seemed to be numb—not capable of true emotion at that time. *What would we tell our families who were expecting us?* We didn't know whether we should call our families or not. It had to be a joint decision, because if one person called home, all the families would know. Many family members of the 801st were at Fort Stewart, Georgia, ready to throw a big homecoming party on Easter Sunday.

We finally decided we had to call. All we could say was that we simply did not know what was happening.

I called Dave. "I'm so sorry," I said with a teary voice. "I have to tell you, again, that I'm not coming home yet."

"What do you mean? Not today?"

"No. Rumsfeld just extended twenty thousand soldiers for a minimum of 120 days. We're part of that extension. I

don't know any more than that. I'm so sad right now."
I stopped talking, stifled a good cry, thinking *I'll save it for
later when I'm alone,* and then continued. "I can't talk to
Mom and Dad yet. Tell them I'll call later. Don't say anything to Laura. I need to know more before I tell her. I'll
call you as soon as I have more information."

"Call any time. Don't worry about the cost. Just call.
Day or night," Dave said.

"We've all been told that the general will be calling families to officially inform you of this change, as a courtesy.
You can expect a call. Oh, yeah—send my boots back. I'll
call when I know more. I love you."

"I love you, too, DeeDee. Keep safe."

We were able to use the computers at Camp Doha, and
I e-mailed a couple of my army friends who were planning
to greet us at the airport. I had my cell phone, and I talked
to others. From then on, I could hardly keep up with the
communication with friends and family.

I attempted to analyze the situation. There had already
been a high number of casualties early in April 2004, and
I thought the military leaders were just trying to figure out
whether they had enough medical soldiers in the theater.
If I had been one of the decision makers, I might have
done the same thing—holding us in theater. But I thought
that maybe a few soldiers, out of the one hundred of us in
our unit, would volunteer to stay longer. Then the rest of
us could go home.

I knew the military had expectations that the casualty
rate would stay at, or exceed, what had already been regis-
tered as the U.S. government was heading toward the
handover of the government of Iraq to the Iraqis. Our

medical unit was already in the Middle East and had provided medical care for the ever-changing Kuwait/Iraq theater of war since May 2003. We knew how medical care
was done in that theater; now the military was going to
use us to "plus up" their number.

Disbelief could be seen on everyone's faces. Yet no one
was crying. No one seemed angry. Everyone was just
numb. I had expected to be gone for six months. I had already been deployed for fourteen months and had been
overseas for twelve months. Our original orders had said
we could be deployed 365 days, but no other Reserve unit
that we knew of had been deployed for more than six
months at this point. We made the *Stars and Stripes* newspaper later that week for our many extensions.

The next couple of days were a blur. We knew we
weren't needed in Kuwait. We were looking at Iraq as our
next likely destination. Or would we go to Afghanistan?

I remember thinking that soldiers from Iraq always told
us we had it made being stationed in Kuwait. We didn't
think so. We were away from our families; we couldn't go
home; we were taking care of sick patients. We did have
some reminders of home, however: restaurants, an occasional movie, a PX for shopping. And we weren't under fire.

I remembered those soldiers and Marines standing in
line for food. Would that be me? In my civilian life I had
always thought a mystery trip would be fun, but the options here were not great.

During the next few days, the higher command at the
brigade level wanted to know each soldier's Military Occu-
pation Specialty. We quickly collected the requested information and sent it up the chain of command. Within days,

the 801st csh was split into three groups and attached to other units in Iraq. We were to support missions in Balad, Baghdad, and Abu Ghraib.

With this third extension, someone with a sense of humor decided that our unit motto would be "Our mission is to complete your mission."

At times like this, the military becomes one big rumor mill as every soldier tries to get information about the new assignment, the area, and anything else of interest. Rumor led us to believe that Balad, the huge Air Force base north of Baghdad, would be the best assignment, but Baghdad wasn't considered so bad either, because the hospital was in the Green Zone. The Green Zone is a "safe area," in relative terms, where the American Embassy is located, along with several restaurants, shops, and the U.S. Command Control Center. In Baghdad one can get a good meal, shop at the Wal-Mart–sized px, and swim in Saddam's pool.

We realized that an Abu Ghraib assignment would be lousy, and we joked about the poor suckers who would be sent there. The prison had initially housed Saddam Hussein's prisoners, but after the regime was toppled, the U.S. Army took charge. We were told the United States added tents that housed as many as 4,500 enemy Iraqis detained by the U.S. military. Several months earlier, the Army had added a DepMeds hospital to care for the Iraqi prisoners and some of our own soldiers and Marines. The hospital was located in the most dangerous combat area of Iraq, ten miles from the outskirts of Baghdad and five miles from Fallujah. There was nothing to do there but work, under difficult conditions. I shuddered to think I might be sent there.

Orders came for a few of us at a time to be attached to other units in Baghdad, Balad, or Abu Ghraib. When soldiers are attached to another unit, that unit has to feed and house them and meet their basic needs. The parent unit, however, is still responsible for leaves, emergencies, pay issues, and personnel issues. Soldiers refer to themselves as—and feel as if they are—"bastard children" of the unit to which they are attached.

It felt strange to say good-bye to that first group of soldiers who left, especially to Cheryl Proper, who went to Abu Ghraib. We had all been together for so long we felt like part of a family. How many of them would I never see again? A few were excited about finally getting into the thick of the action: they wanted to take care of trauma patients. Others couldn't keep the fear out of their eyes.

It would all have been so different had we not had this extension. I tried to find encouraging words, and I told them all that I would pray for their safety. All the while, deep inside, questions kept nagging at me: *Why didn't I get chosen? Will I be next? Why were soldiers chosen the way they were?* I thought I had figured out how things were done, but I soon began to understand how little I really knew. I felt lost without Cheryl.

About three days after that, another group of soldiers received orders—including Commander Gilles, who went to Abu Ghraib. When he left, I became the highest-ranking officer of my unit left at Camp Doha. I worried about the others. How were they doing? Since I had been their chief nurse, I felt responsible for them.

While we waited for more orders to come down, we received word of a mortar attack on Abu Ghraib. One hundred and twenty people had been killed or injured. We were frantic. I ptayed that Cheryl and the others from our unit were safe.

We couldn't get through to the prison hospital, and no one knew if Commander Gilles had arrived there yet. When I finally got through by e-mail, Sergeant Sharon Fuller wrote back: *It is terrible here. If there is hell on earth, I've just seen it. No one from our unit was injured.*

I was unofficially told that I might be working in Kuwait as a direct liaison between the brigade and our unit command staff in Iraq. A couple days later, two specialists were ordered to fill that role on the general's staff. The rest of us got our orders.

I would be going to Abu Ghraib.

"Lord, keep me safe," I breathed silently as I called home.

The Worst Assignment in Iraq

On April 26, 2004, as I stepped out from the open tail of the C-130 military plane into a blast of heat, a first sergeant, dressed in threadbare desert fatigues, saluted. "Welcome to Baghdad, Ma'am," he said. "You have accepted the worst assignment in Iraq."

At that moment mortar fire exploded nearby and, like everyone else, I threw myself to the ground. Lying there with my face burning against the tarmac, I moved my helmet to the side and peeked out. No one seemed to be hit, so I got up along with the others and scrambled among hundreds of soldiers and Marines, all of us trying to find our bags.

The mortar fire continued, like dynamite exploding, some sounding quite close. *What are the rules here? When do you duck? Clearly, I have things to learn about living in Iraq,* I thought as I followed the first sergeant.

First Sergeant Sullivan had come to Baghdad to transport those of us from the 801st Army Reserve CSH Unit to the Abu Ghraib Prison Hospital. After we found my bags, he immediately began to give me and the other soldiers he had already gathered a no-nonsense idea of what life in Iraq was going to be like.

"Make sure you know how to use your weapon," he said, his words clipped, as we wound our way through the crowd looking for three more soldiers in our unit. "We are all medical folks, but here you are going to have to be ready to shoot to protect yourself and your fellow soldiers. No prima donnas are allowed at Abu Ghraib. No matter what your rank, you will take your turn on water duty. You will man the burning pit, burning biological waste. You will drive trucks in the convoy for mail and supplies. Be prepared. You are going to one of the most dangerous areas in Iraq."

We had arrived in late afternoon on the first leg of our new assignment to join Task Force Alcatraz at the Baghdad Central Confinement Facility's new Detainee Hospital at Abu Ghraib. Eight from our unit, three women and five men, would be stationed there until further notice; we joined soldiers from seven other units who made up the task force.

All was chaos and confusion at the airport. By the time we found our duffle bags and each other, we had missed the afternoon convoy to Abu Ghraib. We would have to wait until morning for the next one.

Baghdad International Airport is a vulnerable but heavily guarded site fifteen miles out of central Baghdad. It is literally a runway with tents. Camouflage netting is set up to protect passengers from the fierce heat of the desert while they wait for their flights.

Military personnel occupying the tents orchestrate all incoming and outgoing passengers. The airport offers no other waiting facilities and no sleeping quarters. Potato chips, beef jerky, ice cream, and soda are sold at the tiny PX trailer. Several portable toilets serve as relief stations. What would we do until morning?

"We'll see if we can spend the night at the clinic. That's our vehicle over there," First Sergeant Sullivan said, pointing to a dusty five-ton truck. "We may be able to eat at the clinic, or we can always have MRES"—Meals Ready to Eat.

He took us to an army medical/surgical battalion clinic just outside the airport. They assigned us a small, dark room, where we set up eight cots for our first night in Iraq. First Sergeant Sullivan would sleep elsewhere.

Looking at the narrow cots set up body to body in that small clinic room, I thought, *What is a fifty-three-year-old grandmother doing in a place like this?* This isn't the way I had pictured my career ending. I hoped my life wouldn't end here, too.

What would my assignment be at Abu Ghraib? As a nurse practitioner, I had always cared for my patients with sincere concern for their health and safety. The U.S. soldiers and Marines would get my all, but could I care for the enemy with that same dedication?

I was still trying to come to grips with the events of the past few days. We had thought we were going to bring everyone in our unit home safely. Now we were split up and sent off in several directions. I looked around at my battle buddies crowded into that little room, all looking as dumbstruck as I felt. *Would we all still make it home healthy and alive?*

The playing field was level that night, with no privilege in rank that would make the trip any better for me, the lieutenant colonel, than it was for the specialist. Far-off explosions of mortar fire lit the sky in the distance and sounded ominous. In that intense heat—probably over a hundred degrees—I was chilled to the bone and shivering with fear.

First Sergeant Sullivan had done his job well. His drill-sergeant staccato had hit us like a punch. "You will have the responsibility of defending the hospital and the convoy if need be," he had told us. "Your job on the convoy is to keep your eyes open and be ready to fire if necessary. You are needed at the hospital. Your primary responsibility will be taking care of prisoners. You will always have your Kevlar helmet, body armor, and your weapon. Failure to do so will result in disciplinary action."

The others all seemed so withdrawn and quiet. Some were sitting on their cots, some lying on their cots, some walking around, pacing. Was this what they had been like before, and I just hadn't noticed? Or had they changed when their return home was denied? Or were they like me—just plain scared?

We eight were an unlikely group. We had worked together in Kuwait but in different areas of the hospital. Now we knew that survival would depend on trusting each other.

I was not the only one with concerns about our new assignment. Some of the soldiers were talkative, and some were not. Communication Sergeant Henry Hanson, a personable man who, like me, was a little older than the average soldier, went directly to his cot and lay there smoking one cigarette after another without saying a word. He seemed a world away from the rest of us. *What is he thinking? How is this affecting his life at home?* As closely as we lived and worked together, most of the time we never asked each other about our civilian lives. After a year together, I didn't know these soldiers well at all.

Sergeant Coffman, a newly promoted supply soldier, was worried that he might have to use his weapon. He had been through a year of war without being wounded or having to kill anyone. Now, in this dangerous area where we were going, would he have to kill? Was he ready? Was he able? He kept repeating, "Oh, man!" and his face reflected the fear he expressed so openly.

Major Helen Finch, another nurse practitioner, had initially protested the most about being extended and sent to Iraq. Now, although she still voiced her objections, she seemed to be doing well on this journey.

Young Specialist Baker, a huge, strong man, was suddenly showing more confidence than he had displayed in the year we had been together. It had been easy for many in our unit to take advantage of his low rank and his gentle manner. He worked hard and never complained. I had always been able to talk freely with him about almost anything. He seemed so different to me as he organized himself for the next part of our journey. Now he seemed to exude self-confidence and an eagerness to prove himself in a new location with new battle buddies.

We all ate MREs and then wandered around the clinic by ourselves, deep in thought. Overall, there was a calm, controlled atmosphere in the group. We were respectful of each other, but talk was limited.

I found a computer to e-mail my family, to let them know I was safe. I wondered how they were all dealing with this latest change in plan. Dave didn't say much, but he always voiced concerns for my safety. Laura just wanted me to come home. I sent Laura a brief note: *I am in Bagh-dad. Will convoy to Abu Ghurayb later. Don't worry about me. I'll e-mail you when I get there. Give Dad a hug for me. I love you. Mom.* She would call Dave with the message.

Later that night, trying to sleep on my cot, I watched the light from artillery firing into the night sky. It gave me my first inkling of what life would really be like at Abu Ghraib. I couldn't help thinking about home, longing for my own bed with my husband at my side.

I slept little as I waited for the sun to rise. I knew we had to get up early to catch the convoy for the trip to the unknown. I grimly realized that this unplanned night in Baghdad was giving all of us a few more hours to acclimate ourselves to what lay ahead.

We got up early for our "last supper," as First Sergeant Sullivan called our breakfast. He was treating us to a meal at the "best dining facility in the area." That turned out to be the Bob Hope Dining Facility, located near the airport. It was indeed impressive, with its red and white checkered tablecloths, grills for making omelets, and kiosks with fruit, soda, and juice.

While we ate, First Sergeant Sullivan continued to drill us on the dos and don'ts of life in Iraq. He looked tired as he briefed us very graphically about the mortar attack: the destruction of prisoner tents and buildings, the dead and wounded at the hospital, what the explosions are like, what they do to the bodies, policing the area to pick up body parts. He also gave us the full reality of daily life and survival at Abu Ghraib. His final words of warning were, "Know how to use your weapon. If you do everything I say, you'll have a 95 percent chance of getting out of here alive."

On that happy note, we headed out to the convoy.

Convoy

The convoy consisted of both military and non-military vehicles. That surprised me. American contractors drove their own vehicles, and drivers in western or traditional Arab dress drove the fuel tankers, food trucks, and other vehicles that provided service and supplies to the combat zone.

Some of the drivers waiting in the convoy looked bored, as if they had been doing this for some time. Money must be the magnet that brought them to work here. I thought it must be difficult being here without a sense of doing this for a purpose.

Before long I was standing next to a five-ton truck with slats on the sides of the truck bed, getting ready to pull myself up into it for the first of many times to come. With a twenty-eight pound vest, three-and-a-half pound helmet, weapon, ammo belt, and rucksack, I was carrying about thirty-eight pounds of equipment. I hooked my foot into a little section of the tailgate (about shoulder height to me— I'm five feet four inches tall) and hoisted myself up into the bed of the truck with all that weight on my back. It came clearly to me in that moment why I had to be in such good physical condition. Yet I couldn't help but think that if I had lost twenty more pounds on that Desert Diet Plan in Kuwait (our name for the constant sand in the teeth and heavy hydration), this would be a lot easier.

We were told we would be moving through an area often targeted for attacks and would have to travel with our weapons loaded and aimed out the sides of the truck, ready to fire if necessary. My handgun provided little protection. There were four of us on each side, and I seated myself between two soldiers with powerful M16 rifles.

My weapons training had been the same as every other soldier's basic training, but at that moment I had doubts about my ability and skill with a weapon. I didn't feel ready for a combat zone. As medical personnel, I had never had to use my weapon, nor did I think I ever would. What if I had to kill someone? I was dedicated to saving, not taking, people's lives.

Ever since I realized I might be sent to Iraq, I had practiced pulling my weapon out and putting in the clip every chance I got. Now I had to start handling my loaded weapon for real. *Can I do this?* I wondered. When it came down to the real deal, I especially didn't want to hurt myself or someone near me.

Specialist Baker was sitting next to me. "Specialist Baker," I said. "Please watch me load and unload my weapon. Make sure I'm doing it right."

"Don't worry, Ma'am. I'll take care of you," he said as he watched me load and unload one last time. He nodded in approval.

Then we waited.

Vehicles kept coming in. Some were Humvees, some five-ton trucks, some fuel tankers, some white Suburbans filled with contractors, all heading in the same direction. There were about forty vehicles altogether in the convoy, all of us hoping to get from Baghdad to Abu Ghraib safely.

The convoy commander was organizing the vehicles in the order in which they would travel. Every sixth vehicle or so was a Humvee with a gunner who turned in a pivoting seat just above the vehicle's roof.

About an hour after we had arrived at the convoy location, the commander waved us in behind a fuel truck. *Oh, great! If we're attacked, and the fuel truck explodes, we're dead as well.*

Before we took off, the drivers got together. They went over an intelligence report about what had gone on during the previous days. Did they suspect high danger? Was something blown up within the last day? Then the drivers huddled together to pray for the safety of the convoy.

When our driver came back, he said, with a New Jersey accent, "This is a dangerous road. You are all responsible for defending this convoy. This means everyone. Yesterday there was firing from the mosque about five miles out, so you guys on the right side be especially watchful when we get to that area. Watch the ditches for movement. Watch for suspicious cars, people waiting along the highway. Be alert if it seems especially quiet—that can be a sign of impending attack."

We were all soldiers, but most of us were medical personnel and had never had to use our weapons in a combat zone before. We all tried to look as if we were up to the task, but I wondered how many of the others were as nervous as I was. I tried once again to find a comfortable position amid my gear. At least we were finally moving.

At this point our weapons were not loaded. As soon as we went through the checkpoint, we were supposed to load them. Was this the time? The *click-click* of troops pulling back the charging handles on weapons up and down the convoy gave me my answer.

"Specialist Baker, watch me again. Make sure I have done this correctly," I said. With his eyes on me, I pulled a clip from my vest, loaded my weapon, and chambered a round. I looked up at the big teddy bear of a man for reassurance. I didn't want to be the woman who screws up—the officer who does something stupid.

"You did just fine, Ma'am. Don't worry. I'll take care of you," Specialist Baker said again. His confidence comforted me.

We turned off the paved highway onto a tooth-jarringly bumpy gravel road. My stomach went up into my chest, and my chin kept hitting the top of my vest. Everything jerked around in the back of that truck, and all of us were trying to stay seated on our duffle bags, but we kept banging into each other. To avoid any improvised explosive devices (IEDs) that may have been planted in the roadway, and also to present a more difficult target for mortar or sniper fire, the convoy zigzagged sharply along the most dangerous stretches of the road. At times we bounced two feet off our bags, our helmets sliding around on our heads as we tried to remain upright, hang onto our weapons, and keep them pointed out the side. Without the safety strap across the back of the truck holding us inside, we could literally bounce right out of the truck and onto that jagged gravel road.

We let out collective groans as we continually bounced around in the back of the truck; conversation was impossible. A pair of tanks roared up and down on each side of us, protecting the length of the convoy. At every overpass, one rolled up the overpass and the other stayed down to make certain we got through safely. Then they were both alongside us again, providing a disjointed sense of security. We passed burning and burnt cars, reminders that every stalled car was a potential bomb. Ordnance disposal soldiers and Marines at the front of the convoy decided whether to stop the convoy or pass the car.

Syncopated whirring from an Apache helicopter hovering overhead, watching for signs of attack, was deafening. We had been issued earplugs and had been told to wear them, but I was so scared that I might miss hearing something important that I didn't. Hot, heavy, exhaust from the truck was blasting toward us just above the cab, and our noses were filled with the smell of dust and that exhaust. Between the constant jiggling and the impending doom, I wasn't sure whether I felt more like a bobblehead doll or a sitting duck.

I looked around at the others and knew that they felt, as I did, that this was unreal—that they, too, felt numb. Still, I wanted to take it all in—the scenery, the sounds, the action around me. This was a moment in my life worth remembering. I studied the palm trees swaying amid distant settlements. I memorized the small, nondescript white and sandy-colored houses made of stone or concrete, mostly ramshackle and falling down, dotting the countryside. Then my eyes rested over wide-open spaces until, again, I saw farms with little plots of land, complete with irrigation.

The farmers were growing wheat, corn, and huge sunflowers, which waved in the breeze. The crops looked full and robust. The sunflowers reminded me of the North Dakota plains. An occasional Holstein-looking cow grazed in the distance, and little boys sat out herding cows or goats. We were in the Fertile Crescent, the breadbasket of civilization, and I closed my eyes for a moment to think about that. Without the noisy, dusty convoy driving through it, this would have been a serene scene.

We passed a little boy of six or so who looked as if he had Down Syndrome and a little barefoot girl with tangled hair wearing a red and white dress. They waved to us, and several of the drivers threw fruit, bags of chips, and candy to them. I later learned that the two stood there every day. Although no one had talked to this girl, the drivers had named her Little Rosie. A woman, probably their mother, stood in the distance and watched. Other children, dressed in jeans and pants, sweaters and T-shirts, stood alongside the road in other places, waiting for food they knew the drivers would throw to them.

A few people walked along the road without even looking up to acknowledge this noisy rumble going past, as if such convoys were a normal occurrence. The men wore jackets (*kote*) over long white gowns (*dishdashah*) with headcovers, and some had turbans (*keffiyeh*). The women wore long black *abayas*, with scarves covering their heads.

At intersections, local traffic must stop to let the military convoys through. Queuing up a convoy can take hours; once they start moving and until they reach their destination, convoys never stop for anyone or anything, unless they suspect a bomb in their path. It is too dangerous. If people do not stop for a convoy, they are considered enemies and they may be shot. Even if a child ran out in the road, the convoy would not stop.

At every intersection we saw many small, old cars that looked as if they had seen better days, filled with Iraqi citizens who were forced to stop and wait for the convoy to pass. It probably was a daily occurrence for them, and they looked annoyed and angry. They were giving up their time and space to us, and they had no choice. It made me feel like an intruder, and I wondered how I would react if the roles were reversed.

We finally arrived at Abu Ghraib Prison. Traffic was stopped on both sides of us. Not too far down the road we could see the village of Abu Ghraib. Protesters were milling around carrying signs written in Arabic, and there was general confusion in the area. We drove through a gate, the one with the towers and wall that surrounded the prison, where Marines guarded the first checkpoint. I still could not see anything that looked like a prison building.

As we entered the secured compound, we cleared our weapons. This was the first of many times I would go through the routine as I entered camp or any building on the compound where clearing barrels were placed. Put your weapon on safe, drop the clip holding the ammunition, unchamber your round, put the ammo in your pocket, pull back on the chamber, point your weapon into a clearing barrel of sand, pull the trigger. There should be no live fire into the barrel or disciplinary action could fol-

low. Check your weapon and put it on safe again. This was
to make certain we did not have loaded weapons where we
didn't need them, so we would not accidentally shoot ourselves or anyone else.

Still another dirt road. As we drove on, I kept looking
for the prison and the hospital. Yet another gate, this one
unguarded, and suddenly we came to a stop in a colorless
area near a cluster of buildings. To the left was a collaps-
ing structure with holes in the roof. A fifty-gallon burn
barrel sat near a few other buildings. To the right was a
brick building surrounded by razor wire. Both a Red Cross
and a Red Crescent were painted on the door. *Oh my God!
That's the hospital?*

An open shed that reminded me of an old falling-down
barn had boxes of MREs stacked inside. A hot stench made
me feel momentarily disoriented and nauseated.

As I disembarked from the back of the truck and
looked around, I felt as if I had left the world as I knew it.
This was a different planet—one devoid of life. Ugly, broken-down buildings riddled with mortar fire—not much
more than rubble—stood in the oppressive heat of midday. Reality set in. This had been Saddam's infamous
prison, where thousands of Iraqis were held before they
disappeared. *Am I really here? I don't want to be here!*

Just beyond the razor wire encircling the hospital was
Ganci, a sea of tents housing prisoners within a second
row of razor wire. I could have stretched my arms and
touched the back door of the hospital building with one
hand and the fence surrounding the tents with the other.
A couple of young Military Police (MPs) stood at the entrance to the prison camp, and prisoners moved around—

just wandering, with no apparent place to go. *They are so close!*

Across the front of the hospital building sat three big metal boxes that I recognized as iso units, rigid-wall shelters built into standard shipping containers (known as Isotainers) that are erected on site and used as offices for X-ray, lab, and dental work. Each had a Red Cross marked on its front. On one side of the building were several portable toilets, and on the other side was a small white building and storage tent. A concrete ramp led to the sliding steel door with the Red Cross and a Red Crescent I had seen. Painted next to them were the words "Task Force Alcatraz."

As I walked toward the hospital, soldiers were still searching the ground for body parts that hadn't been picked up after the recent mortar attack. Putrid gray water stood in pools next to the kitchen where my food would be prepared.

The horrible smells are hard to describe and harder to forget. Someone later told me that they were from the bodies buried in the landfill in Saddam's day. I heard speculation about numbers—hundreds, thousands—who knew? Or it could have been the lingering smell from the stacks of bodies that had been piled high in the shower room after the mortar attack only days ago. Old bodies plus new bodies—a smell of death invaded my nose. *Get a grip! Learn to deal with this!*

I again cleared my weapon at the hospital's clearing barrel and walked through the razor wire gate, up the ramp, and into the dark cavern of the hospital. After my eyes adjusted, I could see a desk manned by the soldier who controlled and accounted for everyone who came and went. A few feet beyond the desk was a room that looked like the administration area. It had telephones; in army language it would be called the TOC—Tactical Operations Center. The rest of the area was filled with tents, which would make up the hospital care center, EMT (Emergency Medical Treatment Center), and surgery. I began to feel a little more oriented because the hospital was a standard army DepMeds tent hospital, modified for this environment, with tents set up inside a former warehouse—a building with cement walls, relatively safe from mortar attack.

I went back outside to continue exploring my new surroundings. Other buildings on the site included a dark and gloomy cellblock, called the Hard Site, where Saddam had held his prisoners and where the U.S. military now held high-value prisoners. I was simply told not to go near it. Just down from that, an execution wall and a torture chamber used by Saddam's guards stood glaring in the hot sun like grisly apparitions. The many new bricks used to repair the badly battered surface of the execution wall gave testament to horrors of the past. Colorful artwork painted on the buildings included pictures of Saddam, blotted out with dripping red paint. Those paintings provided the only color in that otherwise drab compound.

Behind the hospital were rows and rows of tents behind razor wire with more than 4,500 prisoners standing inside the hot, dry, dusty area. I could see them, and they could see me. Shivers ran across my shoulders and down my arms.

I swore, then prayed some more.

5

Mortar Attack at Abu Ghraib

Okay, I thought, *this is home for now.* Like it or not. Soldiers can make a home anywhere, and I wanted to find my own space in this God-forsaken dump. I began to look around for familiar faces, my military family, who were already here. They would provide some orientation and show me to my quarters. Then I wanted to find a place to e-mail my family, to let them know I had arrived safely.

As I neared the Tactical Operations Center, Cheryl Proper strode quickly toward me. I recognized her brisk walk and heard her southern twang as she welcomed me from a distance. She looked like she was already adjusting to this new assignment, although she had arrived only two days before the terrible mortar attack. We had been separated for only a few days, but it seemed longer. We hugged like the close friends we are.

She gave me a tour of the compound. This place was hard to figure out. I had no sense of direction, and everything seemed disordered and illogical, like a jigsaw puzzle with missing pieces. It all looked so depressing, like people were just surviving and not really living—in sepia tones instead of Technicolor. They moved slowly and with an aura of doomed resignation. Civilians from countries such as Pakistan, Sri Lanka, and the Philippines—"third-country nationals" hired by Kellogg Brown and Root (KBR) to work in food service—sat smoking in front of small trailers clustered near the kitchen, wearing casual native dress.

Few signs of soldiers or vehicles showed in the camp as we moved from building to building. Cheryl explained that people went outdoors only when necessary, because of the danger and the weather. She stood, as usual, with one hand on her hip. "We could be killed by a mortar round just walking across camp."

Our standard army tent hospital was set up inside the old building for protection. Even some of the hospital buildings were partially demolished, with huge holes in the roofs. While most of the patients were Iraqi prisoners, there was a separate section for Americans who were either recovering from an illness here or getting ready to be transported to Baghdad.

My tour of the place didn't take long, and we went in search of my new living quarters. Unfortunately, there were no designated sleeping quarters for those of us coming in, so I was assigned a hospital cot. I stashed my gear under the cot and followed Cheryl to the one computer available to all personnel. After what seemed like a long wait for my turn, I e-mailed my daughter and my sisters to assure them that I had survived the convoy. Then I met Cheryl for dinner in the chow hall to talk some more. I asked about the mortar attack.

"It was the worst attack here ever," she said. "The whole thing is kind of a blur in my mind, but I will never, ever, forget that day." Cheryl's words tumbled out quickly, as they always did, but her voice had a flatness to it that I hadn't heard before.

"It started out as a pretty quiet day, no different than most days here. Since I was new, one of the officers asked if I wanted a tour of the area to get my bearings. I agreed without hesitation. We went to Ganci. I was so shocked, like you were, by how close the prisoners are." She stretched her arms out to each side. "It was about fifteen minutes after I came back from the Ganci area. I was just ready to start my shift in EMT when I heard the first blast. Within minutes, word came over the headquarters radio that Ganci had been hit—and hit bad. I couldn't believe that I'd been standing there only fifteen minutes earlier!" Cheryl took a deep breath and looked at me with wide eyes. I put my hand on her arm. Then she continued.

"The explosions kept blasting away and soldiers and Marines started coming to the hospital entrance. I went outside to start triage. Colonel George ordered me back inside until the shelling stopped. I said, 'I'm not leaving these soldiers and Marines,' and I just continued. It was chaos—just chaos. Everyone with an injury felt like they needed to be admitted. But you know the drill: triage into the areas of immediate, serious, minimal, and expectant." Cheryl pointed to different areas for emphasis.

"Most of the cases were respiratory distress and chest and abdominal wounds. Before long I saw Colonel George outside, too. I know I remained calm through all of it, but I remember thinking, this is really combat."

She took another deep breath. "After the mortars finally stopped, we had worse chaos. The injured started coming on foot, carrying other victims in any way they could. Trucks and Humvees brought in truckloads of injured. Our area was filled with both living and dead bodies. We were all covered with blood, and the bodies began to smell in the heat.

"Colonel George took charge. He directed soldiers and Marines to where we had set up triage, and several medics and nurses helped in that area. We didn't have enough beds for all the injured, so we called in helicopters to start moving those who needed to go to Baghdad. Oh, Deanna, it was such a terrible day!"

She picked up her fork as if to begin eating. "I've been trained to triage patients over many years for just this kind of disaster. But I've never had to put someone in the expectant category before. They were dying, and the only comfort we could provide was to let them die. That was so hard."

She put down her fork again and shaded her eyes with one hand. Her voice broke. "Some of the prisoners were bleeding uncontrollably. Others had their abdomens or chests blown open. All we could do was cover them and dispense pain medication. We assigned soldier medics to care for them. Those poor people!"

Cheryl wiped a tear from her face. I began to wish I hadn't asked her about this.

"I didn't know what to do with the dead. That day was so hot, like always, about 120 degrees. The smell was so awful. I decided to put the bodies in the room we use for prisoner showers, thinking we needed to get them out of sight and out of the sun.

"But the response from around the compound was unbelievable, Deanna," Cheryl continued. "Off-duty soldiers came to the hospital to help. We assigned them to run for supplies, transport, or anything else we needed. That was such a big help."

"You must have been exhausted," I said.

"Yes. It was about seven hours before any of us were able to even take a breather. In spite of everything, it really was well organized. But I hope I never have to go through that again."

Twenty-two prisoners from Ganci died, and ninety-two Iraqis and Americans were injured. Fortunately, no American soldiers were killed. The pain and fatigue on Cheryl's face made it easier to understand what a terrible physical and emotional toll it had taken on her. All the others here were involved in it as well. I needed to remember that.

But the thing that kept coming back to my mind was that Cheryl had been standing within the target of the attack only fifteen minutes before the first blast that hit Ganci. *I had almost lost my best friend and battle buddy.*

The next day I was ready to report for my shift as staff nurse at the hospital. I did not have a leadership role since we were attached to a unit already there. That was fine with me. I wanted only to be a valuable addition to the staff, to make a good contribution to the mission. Several weeks later, based on military rank, I was made nursing supervisor.

I walked past the grease board sign that read, "Happy Birthday Specialist Taylor!" On another part of the board, a message requested volunteers to join the church choir.

Another announcement in bold red letters started out: "Organizational Meeting." I didn't read the rest.

I entered the EMT ward, where there were eight cots lined up, and emergency equipment stood ready for use. I was surprised to see red biohazard bags taped to the standard hospital floor. I asked a young nurse about it, and she explained that the bags covered a floor soaked in blood during last week's attack; they hadn't yet been able to get replacement flooring.

My next surprise was the soft chugging of a shiny cappuccino machine—the real thing, like a coffee shop would have—in the corner of the ward. The lieutenant sitting next to it saw my delighted smile. "I managed a coffee shop back home," he told me. "My coworkers sent this to me."

Even a few creature comforts can make the unbearable bearable. This coffee would be my sense of home away from home—my comfort and pleasure—in the months to come. The smile remained on my face as I continued back through the dark open area where I had first come in, turned right, and entered the Intermediate Care Ward where I would be working.

The ward was a standard twenty-cot tent, and all the beds were filled. Twenty faces turned to look at me as I slowly walked between the cots. They were not American faces. The forty eyes that followed my every move looked as curious about me as I was about them. Each man was restrained to his bed by one arm and the opposing leg—if he had one. At the front of the ward, two armed MPs stood guard, watching the patients attentively for any unusual activity. We were told to be vigilant: a prisoner might try to harm us.

The nurses' station at the end of the ward included two dusty, gray, metal desks, a white fiberglass sink without running water, and a walkway to the outside of the tent where supplies were stocked. One locked cabinet held drugs, and one unlocked cabinet held bandages, IVs, and other hospital supplies.

Beyond a brown canvas door was the smaller section for the few injured U.S. soldiers in our care. That was also where we would eat, at a small table in the corner. *Where would we sit to chart or give a report to the receiving shift? Where could one go to have a moment of privacy to think?*

Such a dirty place. Everything was dark and covered with a film of grimy dust. The floors were covered with worn and heavily stained canvas; the ceiling housed bats, which flew around the heads of the night shift. Everything was fashioned from crude, raw wood, and clutter was everywhere. How could we prevent open wounds from getting infected in this filthy place? I couldn't help but think about my own health. I hoped my appendix would not fail me now. I sure didn't want to have surgery in a place like this.

The last time I worked in a hospital ward was in the old barracks hospital at Fort Gordon, Georgia, in 1971. Twenty pairs of eyes had looked at me, wanting help, but they were all American soldiers, back from Vietnam, and I was about the same age as they were. I was young and naive, ready to take on any task. That hospital was a clean, well-organized machine.

Now I had come full circle, and I hoped I was up to this mission. Although I had spent fifteen years working in Intensive Care, it had been much longer since I had been a staff nurse in a hospital. I would have to remember how to set up blood transfusions and ivs, to wrap amputated limbs, and to care for extensive wounds. In some ways, returning to this bedside nursing was bold new territory for me at this time in my career.

How would those skills, last used years ago, serve me in this next phase of my nursing career?

Living in the Shadows

That first day of work, I was assigned to care for a seriously injured patient who had just been moved close to the nurses' station from the Intensive Care Unit. Bassem, an Iraqi man in his late thirties with a long, thin body, had been shot in the head and left for dead.

His injuries and subsequent neurosurgery had caved in the right side of his skull. He had an open hole in his head that continued to ooze fluid, and we were sure that, as hard as we tried, we would not be able to prevent infection. I expected that he would die.

He was disoriented and agitated. His left side was semi-paralyzed, but I soon found out that his right arm and leg were very strong. He was a shopkeeper who lived in Baghdad, but no one knew how he was injured or who found him.

The biggest challenge was just trying to keep things clean. We had to make certain concessions, given our situation, and storing things on the floor and under the bed was one of them. Reusing things was another, and trying to make bandages last just a little longer yet another. We often ran short of clean linens, so we turned the sheets several times before we finally had to change them.

Bassem required continual care, and rarely did he stop moving and pulling on his various tubes. He had an IV, a feeding tube going into his stomach, and a urinary catheter. At the end of my shift, I was exhausted from monitoring his constant movement, repairing his torn-up bed, and cleaning up after his constant diarrhea, brought on by the tube feeding. I had to haul water from outside and dispose of the dirty water in the outside porta potty.

Bassem gradually become stronger and more alert. With the help of a translator, we learned that he was becoming more lucid. He asked where he was. Although he was still confused, he became less agitated. We started getting him out of bed, and we learned how set he was on defying the odds.

We had no physical therapists, but we did physical therapy with him. His left arm became stronger, and one day, when we were not looking, he somehow got out of bed and was standing on both legs, an MP next to him with weapon in hand. Soon he was trying to walk with a crutch. We moved him into a regular ward, where he thrived and became more mentally alert.

Bassem was a bit of a mystery to me. I never really knew how I felt about him. Was he an innocent, or was he involved in a fight against the Americans? I know in my heart what I think is the truth. But it really didn't matter what I thought, because my job was to take care of him as best I could. My nursing code of ethics required that I respect all human dignity; place my primary commitment on my patient; and protect the patient's privacy. The military and the Geneva Convention both require that we provide the same life-saving treatment and care to prisoners as we do to other patients. Therefore, I gave each patient my best, no matter who he was.

Seeing Bassem get better was rewarding for all of us. Maybe because we were saving a human life, and maybe because he showed how skilled we really were, not only at keeping people alive but at giving them another chance at a normal life.

Bassem stayed at the hospital a little over four months. He said he had a wife and two children and he was ready to do anything to get back home. When he left the hospital and went to Ganci, I think he was banking on getting out of there quickly. The liaison officer, a representative of the military magistrate's office who spoke Arabic, would help him with application papers for an appeal.

I often wondered how he was doing, but I did not worry about him surviving after what I had seen. He was a true fighter. I am not sure if we changed his heart and mind by treating him with dignity and kindness, but if he is alive now, he must think about us once in a while.

Some of the soldiers in our group were housed in Tejada, the men's building named after a soldier who died there. Getting to Tejada required a walk down Sniper Alley. More hits had occurred in that open area than anywhere else in camp, and I never visited the place.

After a few days of sleeping on a hospital cot, I was offered a space in cellblock F, a section of Saddam's old prison that the soldiers had named the Shadows. I would

be living in the Shadows with Marines and Air Force personnel. I wasn't thrilled with the accommodations, but in
comparison to the options, it didn't seem so bad, and I
would finally have my own space. I gratefully accepted my
new quarters. I would just have to get over the eerie feeling about former tenants.

That cellblock had not been occupied since the last of
the Iraqi prisoners were there, and my cell was full of de-
bris. After the workers, third-country nationals on a building crew, emptied it of the stacks of wood and metal, I es-
timated it at about eight by ten feet. It had brick and
mortar walls, a small barred window high on the back
wall, and bars on the front wall. The glass in the heavy,
gray, metal door was broken, and the cement floor was
filthy. Rumor had it that the Shadows was so named because of the ghosts of those who were killed there under
Saddam's regime. I laughed when I heard the story, but
soon I, too, could feel their eerie, but not necessarily
threatening, presence. I just learned to live with it.

I believed my cell had been used for more than one person. A tiny closet at one end, perhaps two feet by three
feet, may have been used for solitary confinement. Its
walls were covered with Arabic writing. I couldn't imagine
a person confined to that small space.

I took a picture of the walls before the workers white-
washed them, so I could have someone interpret the writing. "Mercy is from God indeed. It is not from the tyrant
human being," it said. It listed several names, but the ones
that could be deciphered were Talal, Fauad, and Malaki. I
didn't want to think about what might have happened to
them.

I furnished my cell with a thin woven straw-colored floor mat, my green army-issue cot and sleeping bag, an upturned cardboard box for a nightstand, and a brown canvas collapsible camp chair. Disposable blue surgical cloths over the front bars served to provide a little privacy. I used a flashlight to find a change of clothes.

It was a long time before electricity was installed in the cellblock, and even then it didn't always work. The window air conditioner and my small fan thus provided only sporadic relief. I heard noises from the many women who lived within a few feet of me, in a windowless room just across the walkway. Of course, we all kept very quiet because we worked different shifts and someone was always sleeping. I occasionally had a roommate, and it seemed she always worked a different shift than I did, so there was nowhere to go during free time.

The showers were located near the Shadows, and rules of the compound allowed us to run there without our gear and run back. We could leave our brick-and-mortar prison area, go down an enclosed walkway of about thirty feet, and then cross an open courtyard that was used for a basketball court. The showers were in a small trailer just beyond the open area.

I had a home of my own again. I spent as little time there as possible.

The Shadows, situated closest to the perimeter, endured the worst of the daily mortaring. We went to sleep most nights with mortar fire pounding a jarring lullaby into the very ground beneath our cots. Sometimes it came too close for comfort. I somehow learned not to hear it.

All in all I was becoming acclimated to this strange place, learning how to manage on the little that we had. I answered my sister Pat's e-mail:

We have to conserve everything here, every piece of paper, paper cups are used over and over. There may be a run to Baghdad in a few days so everyone can order one thing to bring back. You could send Clorox wipes, Shout packets, squish in a roll of paper towels. We don't see those things here. A small plastic tablecloth, a few Tide tablets. I now use a pail to do my laundry that I need from day to day since you can't depend on the laundry service here. I need some lotion and bug repellent. I have two soldiers requesting a James Bond rocket pack to get us the hell out of here.

Not long after I arrived, I was taking a shower at 10 PM when I heard blasts nearby. A mortar attack. *Is it safer to stay inside this tuna can or to make a run for it back to my quarters?* I was dripping wet in my towel when the sergeant of my ward in the hospital came running with my vest and helmet. I quickly dressed and put them on, and we made a run for it, staying next to the building. We got back to our quarters safely, and no one else sustained any injuries. Damage to the buildings was difficult to assess because they were already so torn up by mortars.

We were all supposed to be with someone else at all times for accountability, even going to take a shower. When there was an attack on the camp, everyone had to be accounted for. For example, after a mortar attack at night, our hospital group at the Shadows had to call in and account for each individual who was not working at the hospital at that time. Sometimes someone would be missing on the first count, and we checked for him or her immediately. Maybe he had missed a convoy from Baghdad or had changed a schedule. We never did have anyone truly missing, but it could be nerve-racking to wait until all were accounted for.

In addition, we were not supposed to be out walking alone at any time, especially after dark—particularly women. The dangers for women were for general personal safety, the same as at home. Occasional breakouts from the tent prisons made it even more dangerous.

During that first week at Abu Ghraib, my mind could not wrap itself around the fact that I was in this dreadful and dangerous place when I was supposed to be home. The unfairness put a hard lump in my chest and a hot flush on my face every time I thought about it. My actions became jerky and my footsteps hard and heavy as I moved about the compound that, obviously, even God had abandoned.

Our camp had no amenities. We had no PX because of the dangers for the Army and Air Force Exchange Service who would have to run it. Food from the prison kitchen was unidentifiable and barely edible. Water and electricity were rarely available at the same time. Being outdoors was too dangerous, so we couldn't exercise, and we always had to wear thirty-eight pounds' worth of full gear when we were outside the buildings.

I tried not to complain, but I did. I missed my husband, my daughter and her family, my sisters, my parents, and my friends. Most of all, I missed my little granddaughter, YaYa, more than ever. Over a year of her young life had passed while I was in Kuwait, and I just wanted to go home. My feelings were out of my control. As hard as I tried to accept the extension and this horrible assignment, I just could not do it with grace. I broke down on the phone with Dave once. "I can't stand it here," I had cried. "I want to come home." Bless his heart, he bucked up and gently told me that he wanted me home very much but that I had to do my job. That was the best thing he could have done for me. It calmed me down.

I just hadn't realized what a really bad situation I would be walking into at Abu Ghraib. The staff had worked nonstop for days after the mortar attack. They were burned out—happy for more help but too tired, mentally and physically, to be friendly. They couldn't help us adjust.

I felt every bit as much a prisoner as those on the other side of the fence. Every day I prayed, "Please, God, just keep me safe today." We may have been only ten miles from the outskirts of Baghdad and five miles from Fallujah, but I felt as if I was a million miles from nowhere.

The Marine and Mohammed

I quickly became familiar with the hospital and the ward to which I was assigned. Our daily work involved a lot of wound care, amputation follow-up care, pain management, and working closely with the patients. We had basic supplies and surgical and emergency room capability, but nursing and medical care presented challenges in this austere environment. We learned to improvise when we ran out of supplies like colostomy bags. That was not easy to do. Without physical therapists or occupational therapists, we had to be creative in finding ways to rehabilitate our patients. We wore many hats and did the best we could.

All DepMeds hospitals are set up alike; for those of us who had not worked in a prison, this lent structure for providing safe and reasonable medical care. The challenge was providing good nursing care while keeping aware of personal safety. The MPs played a vital role in that respect. An MP was always stationed at each entrance to the hospital. Other MPs stayed beside the doctors and nurses as we cared for patients. Translators were always on hand.

Every time we left the hospital, even to use the outdoor toilets, we were required to carry our weapons. When we re-entered the hospital, we cleared them in the clearing barrel, turned them over to the secured office manned by the sergeant on duty, and received a number, like a coat check, for the weapon.

The young soldiers and Marines were impressive. (I had learned many years earlier not to call Marines "soldiers.") They seemed so seasoned, so road smart, so very brave. For the first time, I had a full appreciation of what soldiers and Marines in Iraq were doing. I depended upon them and trusted them to keep us safe. I also finally realized why, when they had come to Kuwait, they always commented on how nice we had it there.

I did a lot of thinking about how I would handle my feelings about the prisoners I treated. I would not get to know anything personal about the patients, I decided, and would not listen to anything about their children and families. I would maintain neutral feelings about them and only treat their medical needs. I would be professional but not personable.

E-mail to my niece, Amy:

This is by far the most unusual experience of my life. We are in such a very dangerous place with such a terrible history and yet I am sitting here tonight e-mailing and there is a movie playing in the background. We all know that at any moment we probably will be mortared but in between life goes on. I wear a helmet, interceptor vest, and a weapon everywhere except in the brick buildings. You just drop to the ground when the mortars come in because the shrapnel rises and injuries are usually less on the ground. If you are within a certain range you just need to kiss it good-bye. We are like prisoners ourselves here. Age and rank have few if any privileges here. The doctors are carpenters when not in surgery, we all have to burn trash and human waste, clean up this place, and you name it. Survival is the name of the game, and everyone has to participate. I will survive this but I do know that I will have survived a little bit of hell in the process.

One evening shortly after I arrived at Abu Ghraib, the front doors of the hospital flew open and a few Marines burst in carrying one of their own. "Where do we go?" they shouted. "Our buddy's shot!"

Immediately, we all dropped what we were doing and ran to the EMT. In a blur of activity and noise, with doctors and nurses asking for this or that piece of equipment, the bloody body in full uniform became the focus of everyone's attention. He had been shot in the head, and much of the back of his skull was gone. His face was covered with blood.

The EMT staff started full emergency care, including IVs. The helicopter was called for the seven- to ten-minute ride to Baghdad, where he could get his chance at life with neurosurgery. All of us knew that would not happen for him. He was injured too badly, and not even the best emergency center in the world could save him. But we were going to try.

More than enough qualified soldiers were doing what could be done, but many of us others could not move away.

We seemed to feel the need to stand guard or protect one of our own. We were all probably feeling a little more mortal.

I looked at his dirty, bloody body, the uniform worn at the knees and elbows, his smallness and thinness as he lay there. I saw the tag with his name and the other one that read "U.S. Marine." He looked so young. *Had I just seen him around the camp? Had we crossed paths? Did he live in the area I lived in?* I wanted to know, but at the same time I didn't want to know. These young men looked so tough and combat-hard in the camp and so vulnerable when lying there as patients.

The Marine was quickly cleaned up, lovingly wrapped in blankets by the nurses, and whisked to the landing pad. It all may have taken twenty minutes.

The next patient came in as he was leaving. He was dark haired, dark eyed, and barely conscious, and he had a bullet wound in his abdomen. U.S. military had found him and brought him into the hospital for care.

He was obviously not a soldier, was likely of Arab descent, and had no identification of any kind on him. He wore traditional dress. The obvious was on all our minds: *Was he the guy who shot the young Marine now dying and on his way to Baghdad?*

The EMT room had not even been cleaned, but the work started all over to save this man's life: the IVs placed and the assessment done. Surgery to remove his injured bowel and stop the bleeding lasted for several hours before he was returned to Intensive Care, where he stayed for several days. After that, I started taking care of him in the Intermediate Care Ward, along with Bassem.

The insurgent, as we believed him to be, was breathing

and conscious but noncommunicative, either in speech or in eye contact. When the interpreters tried to speak with him, he would not respond. He seemed scared, but I could not deduce whether he was angry or sad.

He had a tube in his nose and ivs in his arms. On one of those first days he looked under the covers and realized that he had a colostomy bag hanging on his abdomen. He looked at me and I knew he was wondering about that. I asked the interpreter to explain to him that this is where his bowel will now drain and it may be temporary or permanent, we don't know.

He soon started asking more questions and became more agitated as days went by, angry that he was not getting better faster. The colostomy bag bothered him. We got him up and tried to move him, cut his bushy black hair, and watched for signs that he would get better.

His name was Mohammed, but he offered nothing else at first. One day I asked him where he was from, and he did not answer. I asked him if he was married, and he said, "Yes."

Against my better judgment, I asked, "Do you have children?"

He said, "Yes, two little girls." Through the interpreter he said his wife would be wondering where he was and she would be worried.

A wife and two little girls. How sad for them, I thought, but I didn't say anything.

A nurse standing nearby said, "Well, you should have thought about that, you son of a bitch, before you shot one of our guys."

Mohammed became my patient, and day after day I

cared for him. The smells coming from his colostomy bag were foul, and every time I changed it or emptied it the staff and other patients complained. I knew he felt self-conscious, but we did not talk about it.

I knew something was not right because he was not getting better. I began thinking that he was depressed or felt a sense of hopelessness, and I could understand if he did.

One day as I began checking him, I pushed on his belly and saw that the contents that should be going into his bag were coming out of his abdominal incision. I contacted the surgeon, and he was sent back to surgery. Again he ended up in Intensive Care.

I visited him briefly every day, and I saw the inevitable. He started appearing jaundiced, and he had a fever. He was dying. His surgeon discussed his case with another surgeon in Baghdad and was trying to decide what to do next.

One day Mohammed looked at me and, in a quiet but desperate and now raspy voice, asked through the interpreter, "Am I going to die?"

We looked at each other, and we both knew the answer. All I could say to him was, "I will pray for your wife and children." He nodded slightly. He died the next day.

I thought about the families that suffered in just this one incident. The parents and family of the young Marine who died are still grieving today. I want them to know that he had the best care possible and that he was lovingly cared for and honored by all of us that day. He was surrounded by his buddies and by friends that he never knew. My heart breaks when I see his name on the list of U.S. servicemen and servicewomen who have lost their lives. My heart breaks that he could not be saved. I pray for him and for all those like him who died in this war, in this desert so far away from home.

I think also about the family of Mohammed. I wonder if they ever found out what happened to him. It is hard to say. I hope they are not still wondering if he is a prisoner and coming back home someday. I would tell his wife that we gave him the best care we could. I would tell her that I prayed for her and her two little girls that day.

Did Mohammed shoot the young Marine? None of us will ever know. How did I feel about that? It didn't matter. We did our best for both of them.

Prisoner Abuse at Abu Ghraib

News of earlier reported mistreatment of prisoners by U.S. military personnel at Abu Ghraib reached us a few days after I arrived. Like most of us, I heard the news from family—my sister sent an e-mail asking what was going on.

Reports say the mistreatment went on from October 2003 to January 13, 2004. Most of us were new in camp after the first of January. While some had heard rumors, there was no common knowledge by the average soldier of what had happened here.

Our reaction to the news was like that of the rest of the world—shock, disbelief, and anger. We could get only one or two English-speaking channels on our television, and they were blasting us.

The MPs I worked with every day were as surprised as any of us. It quickly became the main topic of conversation. No one had even heard of Abu Ghraib when we first came here. Now, suddenly, we were in the midst of a definitive moment in this war.

Our families were horrified to know that abuse had

happened where we were. My husband knew I was at a prison, but I don't think he thought I was in any more jeopardy than I would have been in any other area of Iraq. Now things seemed different. More danger was linked to Abu Ghraib. And a stigma was suddenly attached to me, just for being there, that he found himself having to explain away.

Even soldiers from home and abroad had a lot of questions for us. "What the hell is going on—it looks bad for all of us," one soldier friend wrote me.

Oh, what a time we faced during those weeks after the news. We couldn't feel defensive, because there was no defending those abuses. But we felt defensive for our own work. We were battered and bruised by the sensationalism—the accusation by association—the looks, the comments, and the aura of incrimination around us. Our lives as soldiers changed after that. We knew this was a black mark against us as U.S. military personnel. All of us were being judged by the world.

The MPs took the brunt of the attention. War is ugly. The MPs had a difficult job to do. MPs had to keep order at the tent areas housing thousands of prisoners. They, along with others, were responsible for camp safety and prisoner safety. Protecting us as we gave care to patients, doing the tasks that go with it, and staying with patients as they moved from one location to another—they did it all. They didn't like taking the patients to the porta potties, but they did it. Processing in new patients was a difficult task, too. But they did their job as they were trained.

Some of the MPs thought we nurses babied the patients. Some saw us as just being professional, respectful. Some disliked both their job and the prisoners. Some were detached. But now the big morality question mark had come up. *What are we really doing here? How are we doing it?*

Caring for prisoners is an emotionally charged experience. I saw difficulties and challenges within our own medical group, who were considered the most inherently empathetic soldiers in the camp. Some of the nurses and medics simply could not handle caring for prisoners.

It became a time of self-examination, as we all began watching our unit and ourselves a little more closely. We became more aware of others around us. The camp probably housed two thousand military and civilian personnel, but we worked in little clusters. We were all so busy that we didn't have the energy to pay attention to anything other than what we were responsible for doing—and we had been encouraged *not* to ask. But now we began to look around to see who, really, was in this camp.

The first soldiers at the hospital were a mix of active duty—the 67th CSH from Würzberg, Germany, and the 848th Forward Surgical Team from Ohio. In February 2004, with minimal resources and staff, they had started setting up a standard slice of a DepMeds hospital to take care of the prisoner patients and U.S. soldier and Marine patients at Abu Ghraib. This hospital was set up after the abuse at Abu Ghraib had occurred but prior to any public knowledge of it. The staff was now around just over a hundred, up from the initial twenty or so.

In addition to our medical soldiers, we had Marine combat troops who came and went, Air Force troops that did all the construction and maintenance, military intelligence, logistics soldiers and Marines, chaplains, the commander and his staff, the MPs, and the ordnance soldiers and Marines who find and defuse explosives.

I e-mailed my sister Pat within days of hearing the news about the abuse.

The stuff on TV about the prison involved a few soldiers many months ago apparently. It just takes a few to make the news. It doesn't include the good things that are done here every day. The prisoner patients are treated well but people do have attitudes that it doesn't make that much difference if they live or die. They are given quite decent care; you just don't use 8 units of blood on someone when you only have a few and a US soldier might be the next patient.

The press from around the world descended on Abu Ghraib by the busload. *London Times,* Reuters, Al Jazeera, Italian and Japanese reporters—name it and they were there, sometimes as many as sixty at a time, walking through the camp on a very tight and secured tour. They came and left fairly quickly.

Because of the heat, we were normally allowed to do patient "cares"—dressing wounds, helping people with personal hygiene, and other daily activities—wearing our brown T-shirts, without our camouflage blouses. Now the ward masters would come in and say, "We're getting reporters; get your blouses on." In less than fifteen minutes we had yet more visitors intruding.

They were allowed to walk through the hospital and observe, but not talk to, the patients. They could watch us briefly as we cared for the patients. It seemed so unnatural to me as we stood like actors, our patients wide-eyed and wondering what was happening, while the reporters walked through the aisles, examining us. I felt like a monkey in a zoo, and I resented it even more than I realized. I would far rather have had them see us working naturally, doing our good work as usual. Occasionally, I wanted to step out of line and just start talking. Instead, I remained silent. It was pointless to buck the system and the rules.

We felt the disdain and dislike from a great many reporters who toured our facility. Those scornful looks even came from U.S. reporters. One of the only friendly faces I recall was that of a middle-aged British woman who stopped and greeted me with a warm smile. "It is a difficult job you are doing," she said.

As the allegations and pictures continued to be publicized, we started fearing retaliation. We were afraid that the world might not even care. What a demoralizing time for us as soldiers. But we found ourselves banding together and supporting each other and working hard to improve the image of the military there and hopefully in general.

We didn't tell the patients what was going on. They knew they couldn't ask; we knew we couldn't tell. Whether the translators clued them in to anything, I don't know.

Shortly after the news, things changed in that reactive way that a crisis sometimes forces. Sheiks from Ramadi, Fallujah, and surrounding areas were allowed to visit the patients weekly to address any of their concerns. We felt their distinct animosity during those chaotic visits. They swooshed through the doorway in a flurry of gray and light blue robes, pushed past us as we worked, and took over the space in our small ward.

Sometimes an Iraqi doctor accompanied them and checked how we were doing cares. Our translators later told us the prisoners were saying that things were okay, or good, and that they were being given good care. The translators said they thought the sheiks were disappointed when the prisoners said something positive.

Sometimes men (and an occasional woman) from the Iraqi government, dressed in suits, came and talked to the prisoners who wished to get messages to their families or to get their pleas heard. The prisoners usually spoke quietly and seriously. Sometimes they were a bit somber after the visits. I always thought they were worrying about family.

We also began playing the call to prayer for patients, five times a day. Each patient had a Koran, and we would never bother someone with cares if we saw him reading it.

With all the world watching, the U.S. military now began paying a great deal of attention to Abu Ghraib. There was a real scramble to get things right and better. This was a switch, and this is part of why we had to examine our own attitudes.

We also found ourselves looking at the circumstances of our lives at the prison, at the communications and the lines of command and any other aspect that might have permitted such a situation to occur. When I came to Abu Ghraib, I realized that the soldiers here seemed of a different breed, a little independent of the whole, because we had to be, for survival. In the 1800s, when soldiers were

sent to the American West to establish a presence or en-
force law and order, they had bad supply lines and little
communication. They had to figure out how to get business done, with no specific guidance. That was us. We just
hoped the leaders would keep things in control. Perhaps
because of that isolation, when we at Task Force Alcatraz
didn't get the supplies, services, or personnel we requested
from higher command, we felt abandoned.

I wondered about other aspects of our daily life. At
every other post or camp where I had served, I was given
an orientation that told me who was the post commander,
where I should go with problems, how the system would
work. That didn't happen at Abu Ghraib. This may simply
have reflected the realities of serving in a war zone, which
was new to me; we didn't have time for the niceties. But it
was disorienting, and others felt it, too. I knew my immediate line of reporting, but I didn't know who was in
charge overall. If I asked about anything outside the hospital or had questions about who else was in the camp and
what they did, I got vague answers. Of course, I was told to
stay away from the Hard Site and from the buildings
where the Coalition Provisional Authority, the CIA, and the
Criminal Investigation Command operated, because I
didn't have business there or intelligence clearance, and it
was safer not to move around outside. But it affected my
perceptions, accentuating the air of mystery, as if I were
being told not to worry about things that were beyond me.

I did not witness the abuse at Abu Ghraib or meet anyone who did. I have wondered if the hospital where I
served was set up as a response, a way to counterbalance it
by providing better care for detainees. But all of my specu-

lating—about abuse, timing, attitudes, systems, isolation, and even our difficult living conditions—could get in the way of doing my job. Focusing on caring for my patients was more than just my professional priority. It was a way to survive.

Attitude Adjustment

I was still angry and upset at having been extended again and sent to Abu Ghraib. But shortly after I arrived, I received an e-mail from a nurse I had worked with at the Kuwait Armed Forces Hospital. Rose, a very spiritual woman from a province in India, wrote:

> *Deanna, I know you are sad because you have been sent to Abu Ghraib, but you must see that it is God's plan for you. God would not have specifically sent you there if he did not have plans for you to make a difference at that place. He will care for you. You will be okay.*

She was right. I had been grousing and complaining, and I had been so angry. Now I told myself, *Okay, suck it up. Enough already. Rose is right. I need to start thinking about how I can make a difference here.*

After that, I started noticing things I felt needed to be changed. Some of the medics and nurses had no compassion for the patients. I wondered what had happened to these soldiers. What made their hearts so hard? I didn't want to be like that. Was this place so awful? What could I do to make things better?

Most staff members were young medics and nurses with minimal experience. Sometimes they had difficulty acting professionally. One day a nurse or medic would be friendly to the patients, and the next day, tired or preoccupied, he would be short and gruff. But the patients expected to be treated the same way every day. The staff's behavior was confusing for them.

An MP might stand at the foot of a prisoner's bed with anger showing on his face. He would say, in English, words known universally, with no chance of misunderstanding the meaning: "Make a false move, and I'll blow your fucking head off." This attitude and atmosphere was not conducive to good health care and healing. I never saw care withheld, but the actions were wrong. As Americans, we needed to do better and be better, and not just because Iraqi translators were watching.

We needed some rules. I announced: "On my shift these are the rules: No foul language. We will not use the 'F word' or the 'F bomb' in front of patients or translators. We will treat everyone the same and be respectful in body language."

It was not a popular move. Following these rules required identifying one's own prejudices and biases, being honest about them, and daily trying to set standards of care. We had to pull some medics and nurses off the floor to staff supply areas because they couldn't deal with the day-to-day prisoner care.

"The truth changes" is an old army saying, and it never seemed more true than in this ever-changing environment. I had to ask myself, *What rules are we living by today? What level of care are we going to give our patients?*

I soon found out that many of the nurses were fairly new graduates and had only basic work experience. We started to educate the staff on the proper procedure for doing blood transfusions. We had to teach the nurses how to make better patient assessments in all circumstances, even when we didn't have automatic blood pressure monitors and other equipment. We began teaching nurses how to manage acute pain. We improved the organization of schedules so patients got adequate care.

Staff got used to restraining their language, but it was a struggle for some. During the transition, I allowed two uses per shift, and people were very funny about it. They wanted to know if they could bank them for a tougher day.

E-mail to my sister Pat:
Have not been mortared today but the day is not over. We eat prison food, so if I don't lose weight here there is no hope for me. Phone service can be very minimal. I am very tired right now and will write more when I can.

The prisoners in the hospital were interesting and diverse, ages fifteen to seventy-nine. All pleaded their innocence to us. I wasn't so naive as to buy all of that. I knew that many of them were our enemies. Yet I learned to believe in the innocence of some of the others. Many times they would come into the hospital scared, wondering what was going to happen to them.

Some of the prisoners spoke English. Several were generals in Saddam's old army, and they were well educated. We could not talk about anything that would breach security while they were in the hospital. They all watched us closely.

Many times patients asked us, "Why are you so good to us? Why do you care?"

My answer was always, "In the United States, we take care of all people the best we can with the resources we have. I will do the same here. I am not your judge or jury. I will give you the same care that I give everyone."

By now, like others in the prison hospital, I had resolved to try to win over one patient at a time with care and kindness. It became our hospital motto: If we can change the heart and mind of one Iraqi or insurgent, we will try.

Communication with the outside world was extremely important. The hospital's computer room had just one computer, and it worked only some of the time. With more than 110 soldiers using it, just getting to it was difficult. When I did, about every three days, I retrieved my messages and e-mailed my daughter, sisters, and friends. We were allowed only thirty minutes. But I always felt re-energized after hearing from my family and friends and being able to respond to them.

On April 28 I answered my niece, Amy, who wondered what she should send me:

I am writing from Saddam's infamous prison of torture. I cannot believe I am here, 7 miles from Fallujah and the main area of conflict right now. Anyway, there is nothing here—no PX *except for a tiny room where they get various things on the days the roads are open to Baghdad. I could use anything like handy wipes;*

Crystal Light drinks like peach tea, and snacks that
will survive the heat since our mail comes only sporad-
ically. I sent all my things like my lotions and all that
stuff home because that's where I thought I would be
right now. I truly feel like I am in the Twilight Zone. I
will let you know if there is anything else I need. Maga-
zines would be good, too.

Of course, letter writing was a weekly thing. Our mail
went out when the convoys could get through, and mail
call was eagerly awaited.

But best of all were the telephone calls, when we could
hear the voices of our loved ones.

I join the line that snakes around the dirty, broken-down,
mortar-blasted building that houses ten telephone stations. We are all hot, sweaty, dirty, and tired, wearing full
military gear. It doesn't matter. Soon we will hear a voice
from home.

We have all bought international phone cards through
the Internet. Four cents a minute—a real deal. We are allowed to use a telephone several times weekly, providing
the connections are working and we are off duty.

As we shuffle forward, our boots roil the desert dust
and we parch beneath the Iraqi sun. I reach for the water I
carry always. I know I will hear relief in my husband's
voice—relief to know that after two weeks in Iraq I am still
okay. This extension has been hard on Dave, but more
than anything else, he just wants to know that I am safe.

Deep in my own thoughts, I know that time will not allow for all the calls I want to make. Rank knows no privilege here. A large sign above each telephone reads:

Telephone calls—30 minutes

Privates—30 minutes

Sergeants—30 minutes

Lieutenants—30 minutes

Colonels—30 minutes

Generals—30 minutes

THAT MEANS YOU!

Whom shall I call and whom will I have to e-mail? The mood in line is subdued. *Will they answer the telephone?* With an eight- or nine-hour difference in time between here and there, often someone will go into the telephone room, dial their numbers, and leave swearing or crying. No one has answered, or the phones are down again, a frequent occurrence. These calls are that important. We wait all week to hear someone's voice. If they don't answer, we may have to endure another whole week before we can try again.

When soldiers and Marines reach their loved ones, their voices soften—become more like who they really are. They became a spouse or a mother, a son or a dad, a lover once again.

Our minds are occupied as we wait to reach the front of the line, where a soldier stands ready to announce, "Number seven open." We hear the clanking of weapons and equipment as a caller enters a tiny telephone room and tries to fit into a lawn chair wearing all of his gear.

None of us has privacy. The telephones are close together, with small panels of quarter-inch plywood between them. Last week, I heard a young soldier who had never seen his baby daughter asking, "What does she look like? Wake her up. I want to hear her." Then, I heard the emotion in his voice as he listened to his baby from the other side of the world.

It's my turn. The cavelike room is dark, and I squeeze into a plastic lawn chair. I shine my flashlight on the dirty telephone, notice all the doodles on the plywood, and begin dialing the first of the numbers I keep in my helmet. No answer at home.

Next to me is a young Marine talking to his son, trying to teach him how to hit a ball. "Hold the bat real tight," he says as he leans forward, curling his fingers in midair. He swings his arm back and forth and speaks gently and lovingly, "This is how to swing," as he tries to instruct his young son, who is thousands of miles away.

Suddenly he looks at his watch and remembers the thirty-minute rule. He ends the call and sits with his head down for a few seconds. Then he stands, picks up his weapon, squares his shoulders, and becomes a Marine once again.

I dial the next number. Then, listening to my daughter telling me what new things my granddaughter does, it doesn't even matter that mice climb the walls and circle my feet as I talk.

Settling In

In an attempt at beautification and sanitation of the operations at Abu Ghraib, the name of our hospital was changed to Task Force Oasis. Who had permitted that name—Task Force Alcatraz—in the first place? We were full of cynical jokes about what *Oasis* meant. Some energetic young medics tried to transplant a small palm tree to a spot just outside the hospital door, but it did not survive—fueling the cynicism.

We were henceforth to refer to the patients as "detainees." We were told that the camp was going to close and we were to move to Bucca, in southern Iraq, in June.

I called Dave. He had just gotten up, and he gave a quick sigh of relief when he heard my voice. I explained, only briefly, what was going on. We were never supposed to say, over the telephone, where we were or where we were going, for security reasons. I just told him that things were changing and that I would probably be moving. "I can't say when and where, but I'll tell you when I get there."

"Still in Iraq?" he asked.

"Yes."

"Will it be better?"

"No."

"Well, don't tell me if you can't," he said. He never wanted to know too much. "I was at Laura's again last night for dinner," he told me. "And I've been babysitting on the evenings that Laura works."

"I envy that," I told him. "I miss YaYa so much. How is she?"

"She's just great."

"Have you seen any of the neighbors?"

"Tom had me over for dinner one night last week. They're doing fine. And Pat calls often. Pat and Nan both e-mail Laura all the time, and Laura prints out the e-mails for me to read."

"That's good. I call Mom and Dad often. Are my checks making it to the bank okay?"

"Yes, they are."

"Will you do me a favor and buy six shirts that say 'Minnesota' on them, and send them to me, please? They're for the translators."

We had conversations like this because we had no privacy to be more personal. I was still sorry I had been so emotional when I first arrived. That had been really hard on Dave. He was my confidant and support. He always wanted to be a soldier, but since he wasn't, he encouraged me when I didn't have the "Be all you can be" attitude. I always tried to not let on to Dave when I was really feeling lonely. And I know that he, too, protected me from his real feelings about my being gone so long.

Improvements at Abu Ghraib began with the tent areas of the detainees, initiated by a visit from Red Cross International and the U.S. military. Family visits were arranged for detainees, and their food improved. Broken-down buildings were razed or repaired. A chow hall that we dubbed the Mortar Café was installed in the Shadows, right outside my quarters, so we no longer ate from the prison kitchens. During all that digging, the smells and sights got worse as bones and garbage were unearthed. I stopped looking down when I walked outside the buildings.

New water pipes and trailer housing were put into place. I am not sure who recommended trailer housing. Mortars hit and damaged the trailers regularly, so they didn't survive more than a few days.

Journal entry, May 18, 2004:

I'm adjusting to this cursed place. The Shadows is a fitting name for my quarters, as I know ghosts of the past are in here. Should I be more cautious with talking to interpreters? Are they friend or foe? I trust my instincts with two of them and will pursue my friendships. I don't understand what they went through. I want to. I think Iraq is beautiful and could be again someday if it can be restored. Sirens and gunfire tonight. Sirens were testing/gunfire real. Sometimes I'm scared, mostly just going through the motions of living—one foot in front of the other. I have AC and a bug zapper—what more could I want? For the first time in my life I do not feel friendly or like a friend to many, but I really don't care. I just want to survive and go home. I am living like a nun tonight—alone in my cell.

As we waited for what would happen next, insurgents tried to breach our perimeter. One day, an alert Marine noticed someone kicking dirt around something on the ground in the convoy staging area of our compound. He began to investigate, and the suspicious man ran. The Marine captured him, and further investigation revealed that he had been trying to cover up a plastic explosive—a C-4— that he had planted.

Rumors of the incident spread quickly, and any feelings of relative safety we may have had were shattered. I often wondered which of us would have been killed if that explosive had not been discovered. It could have been me.

We were notified that the decision to move to Bucca was reversed. We would be staying at Abu Ghraib. Nothing is certain with the military until it is on paper, and maybe not even then. My boots knew that story.

The sign outside the hospital entrance read "Task Force Oasis." But in spite of our new name, the motif inside the hospital's areas for soldiers, outside the hospital wards, and on the tongues of soldiers was "Task Force Alcatraz." I continued to see shirts with black bars on them that said "TF Alcatraz."

It seemed appropriate.

At home in my tent at Camp Wolf, Kuwait

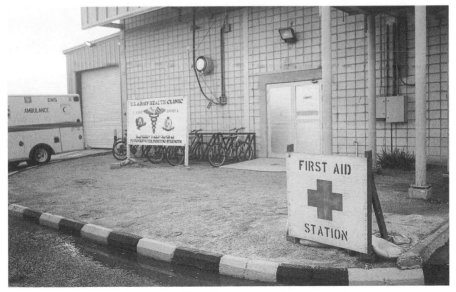

Outpatient clinic at Camp Doha, Kuwait

Loiterers I met on my field trip to the docks at Umm Qasr. They wanted only to have a picture taken; I was nervous enough to keep a hand on my weapon.

*Saying farewell to Atik,
barista extraordinaire, at Camp Doha*

A five-ton truck, our convoy transportation

The south entrance to Abu Ghraib Prison's hospital area

*The hospital building, a former warehouse,
had an unusual roof.*

*Some soldiers attempted to beautify the hospital entrance by
transplanting a palm tree, but it didn't survive. The framing
at left became a platform where detainee patients could get
some fresh air and play dominoes.*

At the hospital entrance.
This stray dog, sometimes known as Iwaki Dog
or just Whacky, became something of a mascot.

A woman soldier passes the clearing barrels near the X-ray, lab,
and dental ISO units outside the hospital.

I passed this area each time I went from the hospital to the Shadows.

Bombed-out buildings between the Shadows and the hospital

The entrance to the Shadows area of the prison

A building in the area of the Shadows. Saddam's face was everywhere.

*At the doorway of my cell, wearing my Kevlar helmet, vest,
and ammunition belt*

*A generator outside this room produced electricity for the Shadows.
The writing at the top of the wall says, "Yes, Yes, Saddam is our leader."*

*The writing on the wall of my cell before it was repainted: "Mercy is from
God indeed. It is not from the tyrant human being."*

The Mortar Café

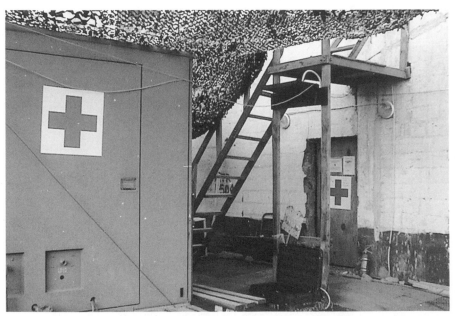

The garden under the staircase near the dental office. A sign saying "Welcome to my garden" sticks out of the back of the trunk that caught the dripping water; someone later added a wading pool and some plants.

Outside the quarters for some of the young medics

Sunrise over the wall surrounding the Shadows;
this was our view on the way to the washroom every morning.

Prince's photographs of central Baghdad included
(left, top)
the Monument of Liberty, erected in 1958 in
Tahrir (Liberty) Square, Baghdad;
(left, bottom)
a street vendor, Mutandol Street;
(above)
a street scene.

In front of one of Saddam's many palaces, this one at Camp Victory in Baghdad, on my best day in Iraq

Lieutenant Colonel Cheryl Proper

Task Force Oasis at the Abu Ghraib Prison Hospital entrance

The comforts of home at Camp Victory

Leaving Abu Ghraib on the last convoy

The last day for the last of the 801st CSH at Abu Ghraib

11

A Day in the Life

Daily life and dangers are different for everyone serving in Iraq, depending upon where they are, but some areas are more vulnerable than others. The experience of a soldier stationed in the Green Zone, the secured area of Baghdad where government officials and coalition administrators live, is very different from that of the soldier at Najaf, Fallujah, and where I was at Abu Ghraib. The soldiers from our unit who were sent to Balad, for example, had trailer housing with privacy, a movie theater, a swimming pool, and all the benefits of living in a large established camp. Danger was ever present at Balad as well, but the hospital at Balad was staffed and equipped better than at an outpost such as Abu Ghraib.

We led a very different life at Abu Ghraib. Our overtaxed generators often failed because of the intense heat, so we lived and worked without air conditioning most of the time. We got water for showers only when the water trucks could run. Laundry service was just starting, but we never knew if we would see our clothes again, so initially most of us washed them in a pail.

We got our mail only if there was a convoy to Baghdad. When the Military Supply Route was closed because of high risk, we were completely isolated by ground. Helicopters dropped drinking water and medical supplies at night on several occasions when things were really bad. We had occasional phone service, using the Iraqi Segovia system; AT&T set up later. The Mortar Café was a significant improvement on the food we had been eating from the prison kitchen.

We had no PX. The soldiers themselves set up a little store with supplies they picked up in Baghdad when convoys could run. My first trip to the PX was a surprise. It held six bottles of shampoo and a few rolls of toilet paper. While it got better before I left, it was never well stocked.

Internet service was fair but not always reliable. We had no Morale Welfare Recreation (MWR). Since the danger was too great to walk outside, we finally got a gym of sorts, with weights, a few bikes, and treadmills.

A day on the ward of the prison hospital at Abu Ghraib started much the same as in any hospital: wake up the patients, record their vital signs (temperature, respirations, pulse, and blood pressure), and get them ready for breakfast. At Abu Ghraib, though, the patients might be insurgents, or Al-Qaida, or innocent Iraqi boys and men; each was secured to his cot by an arm and a leg, and our hands-on care was provided under the watchful eyes of the MPs stationed on the ward.

Sometimes it felt like a daunting task when we turned on the lights and started the day. The detainees were like any other young men—they didn't want to wake up. The morning call to prayer usually got everyone awake and praying, though. Breakfast consisted of tea and bread and occasionally fruit.

Wound and other cares started after that. Amputated limbs, usually legs, were the primary injury we dealt with. Sometimes the doctors wanted to be present for the unwrapping, cleaning, and rewrapping of the wound. Some men had external fixators surgically placed to stabilize shattered bones in their legs or arms; we watched them for signs of infection, cleaning the site where the fixators go into the bone and checking circulation in the limbs. Other injuries included abdominal wounds and gunshot wounds that needed daily cleaning and dressing.

Occasionally we had patients who also seemed to be mentally ill. The language barrier and the prison setting added to the challenge. One detainee looked Arabic, spoke Arabic, acted like a French artist, seemed intelligent at times, and then went into a nonsense mix of words and tirades that at first made people laugh. After a while the detainees told him to zip it, using the Arabic equivalent. We never knew if he was sick or a great actor trying to keep us guessing.

The MPs carried the keys to the patients' restraints, which we loosened for eating and removed for toileting and physical therapy. We checked each detainee's skin regularly to make sure the leather limb restraints were not too tight. It would have been difficult for them to get loose, but it was also nearly impossible to leave the ward, as soldiers were at each exit.

On the days we had outside water available, a few of the detainees would be escorted out for a shower. On other days, simple cleanup at the bedside was all we could manage. Sheets and clothes were changed if they were available and only if needed; sometimes they were only turned over and the soil covered with disposable pads.

The doctors made rounds and wrote orders just as in any other hospital. Some of the doctors were indifferent to the person and others were not, but they were all interested in the health problems. Patients sometimes were quiet and sometimes became boisterous and laughing, depending on the day. We were supposed to limit conversation in the ward, but that rule was never really enforced. In general, these men were very respectful of each other, and certainly age earned increased regard.

My life at Abu Ghraib soon became so routine that my memories blur. It was like the movie *Groundhog Day:* each day was the same as the day before. Sometimes it felt as if all I did was change bandages. I walked down the aisle with my bucket of Kerlix, tape, gauze dressings, Betadine, and bandage scissors, moving from one patient to the next, changing dressings on wounds. While we wished no one ill health, we liked it better with more patients and sicker patients.

Boredom could be one of our biggest enemies outside of work, too. Some of us never got to leave the compound or left it rarely due to the dangers of the convoys. We were creative in making our own fun, however. We had computer games, karaoke, basketball tournaments, Friday night boxing, movies on DVD, and whatever else some energetic individuals and our chaplains could come up with.

My comfort was coffee. I had my own special metal French-press cup that I took with me wherever I went, and

I was methodical about getting and making my good, dark, strong, robust coffee. It tasted of home, and for a moment I could draw a shield around me and make my world very small. Then everything was good.

On May 16, 2004, I e-mailed my sister Pat:

Those boxes just keep coming. I got 1 more today. They have been doing more runs to Baghdad this week. The regular active duty army guys are taking some of their folks to the airport for R&R leave. We just get to stay and run the hospital. They have been in country 4 months at most. Now they are saying some of our people in Balad and Baghdad are not needed and may get to go home because replacements are coming in—but not for Abu Ghraib. Oh well, I can do this for a while and may get leave. You never know. I suppose one day they will tell us just to pack up and go. Got air conditioning today. Watching those guys put it in is something else. It takes forever, and you just hope you won't go up in smoke in the middle of the night. I did give a few of the little bag treats you sent to an Iraqi interpreter from Babylon who has become a friend. He was going home to his family and his little girl. I was standing with the bag of goodies, and I looked down and thought why not. I told him Oreos were America's favorite cookie. I told him to sit down with his wife and have tea when the baby was sleeping and eat Milano cookies. He was so grateful you would not believe it.

I am a private person, but just about everything in my daily life worked against that.

The shower trailers were located behind the hospital and just past the busy dental ISO. When we went for showers in our flip-flops and PTS, we often passed detainees, in wrist locks with an armed MP behind them, coming in for dental care. I didn't want to be seen coming from the shower with wet hair by anyone, and certainly not the detainees. I had no choice.

I carried my shower supplies, towel, toilet paper, and laundry soap in a bucket the size of an ice cream pail. The shower trailer, which was lit inside, had about four sinks and four showers. I do not recall a time when all sinks and showers were operational or when there was not water leaking from somewhere. Often I would go into the trailer, forget that the floor was likely to be wet and dirty, slip, fall, and swear.

I walked down a wooden walkway, set my things on a bench, undressed, and waited for a shower to become available. Only occasionally, on the off hours, did I have the place to myself, and I savored every deliriously wonderful moment of privacy.

Often I went through the whole process, looking forward to the wonderful feeling of getting clean and being relaxed, and started the shower. There would be no water. But water had just run for the last person. What had happened? Either the water ran out or the electricity stopped or the generator that ran the electricity ran out of fuel or— there were any number of scenarios.

I might swear a little under my breath. I would scream and swear a lot if it happened a few days in a row, especially if I was soaped up when the water stopped. Then I trudged back to my quarters and got out the baby wipes. If the power was out, not only did I not get a shower but also there was no air conditioning and no fan, so I would be stinky, dirty, and festering in the heat and dark.

That scenario with no water played out time and again at Abu Ghraib.

Maintaining cleanliness was a constant challenge. We carried our own toilet paper, flattening a roll and keeping it in a pocket. We carried wipes in every pocket. We were dirty, but at least we kept up the effort.

The Mortar Café served at all hours, even 4:00 AM, because soldiers might be going out or returning from patrol. If I opened my cell door even a little bit, the guys serving food could see in. Often they would see me and say, "Madam, come here to eat." Sometimes I thought, *why can't I just get some food and bring it back to my cell?* That would have been too easy. Before getting into the chow line, we had to be in proper uniform, wash our hands at the washing station, clear our weapons, and sign in. KBR had to have a record of how many soldiers and Marines ate so they would be paid.

Unfortunately, I had to cross the chow line to get from my cell to the hospital or the porta potty. My hair might be all over the place from sleeping, but to get to the bathroom in the middle of the night, I had to tromp past a line of soldiers waiting for chow.

Because of the dry climate and intense heat in that area, people could become dehydrated quickly without fluids. We carried big bottles of water with us at all times. It was always warm, of course, bathtub warm, but I would find myself in a panic if I did not have my water with me. Our families sent us Crystal Light or Kool-Aid drink powders to make the water more palatable.

Our backpacks were heavy, even if we were going very short distances outdoors, because we needed, at all times, to be prepared. I often felt like a turtle with the pack on my back and my helmet bouncing around on my head. We could take our helmets and vests off in the chow hall and in the hospital. But we had to have them ready to grab and go.

We were required to be in uniform even on our days off, either our PT uniforms or our brown and sand-colored camouflage uniforms. A person not easily identified as a soldier or Marine could be shot as an enemy infiltrator. Outside our compound, of course, we were always required to dress in our desert uniforms.

We couldn't wear our dog tags in the hospital, to avoid being harmed or choked by a detainee, so we put them in our pockets. But we wore our ID cards in pouches, either hung around the neck or strapped to an arm, and everyone seemed to carry in them a picture of someone special: a spouse, a girlfriend, the kids. When we talked about our families, we could pull out the pictures, and we got very sentimental when we looked at them. Whenever I saw Specialist Baker, I asked him about his girlfriend back home. He patted his pocket reverently with his huge hand and said, "She's still waiting for me, Ma'am."

I also had a Geneva Convention card identifying me as a health care provider. It said I should be released if I were captured. Some thought it would get us a bullet faster.

Your weapon always stayed with you, except when you were caring for patients. I wore my handgun in a holster on my right hip. I carried my ammo pouch in my left vest pocket. I could pull out my weapon, grab my ammo pouch, and quickly insert a clip.

If we were only going to the porta potties right outside the door, inside the razor wire, we were not required to carry our weapons because the hospital was in a wired and protected area. However, many soldiers and Marines brought their weapons with them just in case. Normal bathroom maneuvers are severely complicated by a twenty-eight-pound vest and a heavy helmet. We had some bathroom humor about quick catches made as equipment just about dropped in.

I grew accustomed to having the butt of someone's weapon stick into me, even while taking communion at a church service or standing in line at the chow hall. Weapons always clanked together in the chow line. Marines sat with the butts of their M16s between their legs and the barrels alongside their faces while they ate. The army soldiers, and others, usually laid their M16s by their feet. At first it was unnerving, but it quickly became routine. Weapons and me—never would I have thought that that combination was natural and routine. We just got used to doing everything with our weapons attached.

We faced many dangers at Abu Ghraib. One day, near the end of my stay, Marines with dogs at the gate intercepted a vehicle carrying an improvised explosive device. In a carefully planned attempt, people on the inside of our camp were waiting for the explosives and would have set up a chow hall explosion that evening. The Marines blew up the IED in a controlled explosion, and I shuddered to think that I might have been killed just when it was time to go home, like other soldiers we had heard about.

The Unsung Heroes

Some may argue that the Iraqi translators were not heroes, but that is how I saw them. My job would have been less satisfying and more challenging, and the patient care would have been lacking, without them. They were often courageous, at times afraid, always in danger, but willing, for reasons I cannot fully appreciate or understand, to be there for the patients—and for us.

In our work, as in the war, communication was everything. I had learned to speak some Arabic while I was in Kuwait, and Abu Hani, one of our translators, taught me more when I was at Abu Ghraib. But most of our staff knew little or none of the language of our Iraqi patients. Our translators played a huge role in the medical care we provided.

The translators, who represented the range of Iraq's ethnic cultures, became the most important people in my life at Abu Ghraib. I was lucky and blessed to come to know them as well as I did. They were six intelligent and respectful Iraqi men who collectively worked very hard, around the clock, "to help our Iraqi brothers," as one said.

Each translator had to wear a badge with his real name on it in order to get on to the compound, where he lived for most of the week. But when he left to go home, he hid his badge, so that if he were stopped and checked the ID would not be found. Insurgents placed a bounty on the heads of anyone working for the U.S. military. Even ordinary Iraqis, who considered it acceptable to work for an American or foreign outfit like the electric and telephone companies, would consider them traitors if they were found to be working for the U.S. military.

We never called them by their real names, and I do not use them here. A detainee could get word about them to someone on the outside who could harm or kill them or their families. Just before I arrived at Abu Ghraib, one of the translators and his wife had been killed because he worked with us. The translators each told of ways they kept their lives secret from their families and friends. Working at Abu Ghraib was more dangerous in some ways, they said, but in other ways, it made it a little easier to keep the secret.

An American company located in Baghdad recruited them, giving them a proficiency test before they were hired. As a rule, the better translators were sent to hospitals, because they needed to be able to translate using medical terminology. Their pay took into account the skill level and the danger. A teacher in Iraq earned a little more than $200 a month. Other translator jobs, in other military areas, might pay $440 a month. But the U.S. military paid the translators at the prison $660 a month. In addition, the translators had access to chow and medical services while they were with us.

As dangerous as it was for them, they were loyal to us and helped us in many ways. At times they had problems with terminology, but they worked hard to improve and asked a lot of questions. The work became a calling for some translators who, at great risk to themselves, reached beyond the walls of the hospital to families of detainees.

Abu Hani

Abu Hani was the first translator I got to know. In his fifties, he was the most outgoing, and he had the best command of the English language, in both speech and understanding. He was the leader of the translators at our hospital, representing the group if there were questions about conditions or errors in payment. He was not too shy to ask for more.

In his younger years, Abu Hani had received some education in London, where a brother still lived. I asked him why he stayed in Iraq, why he was not with his brother. "This is my home," he answered. "This is where I need to be." He did not like being poor and living from day to day, but he was willing to do that.

He had earned a science degree of some sort from Baghdad University and had worked as a professional for a while. Before becoming a translator, he had a series of odd jobs that he did not discuss. He told me, "I have no rest when I get home. There are many problems to deal with."

As was his obligation, he had been a soldier in the Iraqi army. He said those soldiers led a terrible life with bad conditions and even worse food. Lots of soldiers deserted, and if they were caught they were killed. He said that if the front lines started retreating during a conflict, the soldiers behind them were ordered to kill them.

When I first met him, he was quite businesslike. He was always dressed in slacks and a plaid shirt and carried prayer beads, which were customary for men to carry and finger whenever they were quiet. He said he was Christian and belonged to a Catholic church in Baghdad.

He was married to a Christian woman and had a teenage daughter and a young son. He was proud of them and worried about them when he was gone. When his wife attended a funeral for her uncle and his two sons, Abu Hani expressed fear for her safety. Sometimes the kids wouldn't go to school for a few days if there was word of problems in the neighborhood.

One day Abu Hani returned from home anxious because a neighbor boy by the name of Nicholas had been abducted. The boy's mother was a widow who could not afford to pay a ransom. The neighbors banded together to try to find him, and a week later Abu Hani said the neighbors came up with the $3,000 demanded for the ransom payment. The boy was returned unharmed.

As the weeks went by, he began to speak more freely. He often said things about his personal life, especially about his wife, just to get a reaction from me. I obliged him, in part to hear his wonderful laugh. We bantered about differences between cultures and men and women. Abu Hani said that he and his wife had a distant relationship; they lived together but grew apart. He seemed bothered by it and joked about it at the same time. That's where Muslim men have it better, he said: The women stay partners in every way, including sexual partners, better than the Christian women who feel they have a choice about these things. He told me he loved his wife, although he had a girlfriend.

He was trying to quit smoking, using Zyban. We talked about stress reduction and aging. He teased me about my age, saying that women in Iraq get old faster (especially Christian women who don't want to be sexually active).

One week I sent gifts for his wife that included lotion and shampoo, and she was thrilled, especially with the shampoo. I found out from several people that such products were almost impossible to come by even if Iraqis had the money to pay for them. A week or so later I sent something else, and when Abu Hani came back to the prison he jokingly said to me, "The gifts are helping me make some progress with my wife. Thanks to you, we had a good weekend." I quickly told him that I didn't need any more information. She sent me some wonderful goat cheese, pita bread, and the best popcorn I had had in a long time. While we were not supposed to eat local food, I took my chance, and all of it was delicious.

His daughter sounded like a typical teenager. She knew about some American movie stars and covered her walls with their pictures. I sent her a few magazines that he said she went crazy over. Often she and her friends could not see each other because the danger was too great to be out of the home. She talked incessantly on her cell phone.

Abu Hani often seemed irritated with his daughter but proud to talk about his home and cell phones. I think he wanted to let me know that he lived a little better life than some other translators. I believe he probably had more money than any of the others. He owned his home and a small piece of land. I always felt he was well connected and knew how to survive.

Abu Hani and I became friends, I think, because I asked if he would be willing to teach me some Arabic so I could talk to the detainees and ask simple questions. He willingly and enthusiastically agreed, and so our lessons began. Each week he gave me twenty words and phrases to work on. He drilled me, and if I didn't study he let me know it. At first I did it to occupy my time, but I soon realized that learning Arabic could be important: I could ask a patient if he was in pain, or needed food or something to drink, without getting a translator.

Overall, I got good marks for my effort and pretty good marks for pronunciation. Later, when I spoke to detainees and they actually understood me, he smiled like the proud teacher he was. At one point he said, "You don't need me anymore."

"You're a good teacher," I responded, "but not that good."

Sometimes I would almost forget that we weren't just friends working together as we would at normal jobs, but the situation quickly reminded me that this place was anything but normal. Abu Hani might even be our enemy. I didn't believe he was—but how could one be sure in this crazy place and in these crazy times?

When he spoke about the soldiers, he was respectful, but he had us pegged pretty accurately. "I know that person doesn't like Iraqis," he would say, or, "He doesn't care about what he does here." He was astute in reading body language and understood more of the slang than the other translators did.

Unlike some of the other translators, he spent time

talking with the detainees when his translating services were not being used. Sometimes I did not know if Abu Hani should be talking with them as he did, but overall I think he was objective in his work with us. He clearly liked people and cared about his countrymen, detainees or not. He wanted us, as military, to make more of an effort to find families and to search more quickly for the truth. Is this a good man or a criminal? That question got answered so slowly.

I was impatient sometimes, seeing men I had cared for who were clearly innocent—people brought in only because they had injuries, for instance, and not because they were a threat to the United States—sitting in that camp, being treated as detainees, waiting to be processed. I could only imagine what Abu Hani must feel. I think I was the safe one to bounce his thoughts off of. I know he enjoyed the friendship of some of the male soldiers as well, but they tended to be less open with him.

Abu Hani's dedication helped a patient detainee we affectionately called Squirrelly because he had a light-hearted personality and said and did silly things once in awhile. He said he was shot in his front yard while defending his family's property. At least that was his story, and we heard lots of them. I took them all with a grain of salt.

Squirrelly had been with us for weeks, and we wondered if his family knew where he was. We asked the MPs to follow up to see whether the family was notified. We got no response. It was more difficult than you might think. He gave a description of where he lived but not an address; the streets in Baghdad had been named just five years earlier, and many people did not know their own addresses.

Abu Hani found the house when he went home to
Baghdad on the weekend. Taking a great personal risk, he
spoke to the family. Squirrelly's parents cried with happiness to find out that their only son was alive. The mother
wanted to give him something in thanks, but Abu Hani
said he was uncomfortable with that and quickly left. He
said the father had searched for his son every day after
work, trying to find word of his whereabouts.

Abu Hani made my life so much better at Abu Ghraib.
I am grateful to have known him and appreciative for what
he did for all of us. He gave me a glimpse into life in Baghdad. I know he may have lived a harder life than he let on,
but he would have been too proud to complain.

Prince

I knew Prince nearly as well as I knew Abu Hani, but he
was a clear contrast. Prince seemed to be a young man
caught between the old culture of Iraq and the new. He
was a Shia Muslim and proud to be an Iraqi, talking enthusiastically about the country's natural richness. At the
same time he was most eager to embrace all that was western—clothes, movies, and especially the Internet. He also
talked a lot about leaving as soon as he could.

Prince was not, of course, his real name, but that's what
we called him, and he loved it. He was about twenty-three,
a graduate of Baghdad University in literature and English. His English was fairly good, and it got better as he
spent more time with us and supplemented his book
learning with conversational English. He took his job seriously with regard to translating but did not go beyond the
basic requirements. Instead of talking with the detainees,

as Abu Hani did, he preferred to spend time with the young soldiers who were more his age. He listened to their casual conversations, laughing and trying to understand and learn the jokes, and he watched movies with them.

Before coming to us, Prince worked with the 82nd Airborne, always moving, always on the run. He also thought they were too rough and tough. He liked working with the medical personnel much better.

Prince was not unlike many young men with regard to his interests—women and anything having to do with technology. I believe he led a fairly sheltered life before going to college. He lived with his parents on a farm north of Baghdad. I got the impression that they were not particularly poor. He showed me pictures of the crops they raised, which looked like corn and grain. We realized that we had things in common when we talked about cows and corn and I let him know that I, too, had grown up on a farm.

He never showed me any pictures of his family or talked about them, except for his mother. He told her he was working at a company rebuilding in Iraq. He said he could never tell her he was working with the U.S. military. She would not be able to live with that. She always told him, "Stay far away from the U.S. soldiers. They will slash your neck if you are not looking." He smiled when he thought about it sometimes, especially when he lived and slept only a few feet away from us.

All the translators were responsible for getting to work and home on their own. Prince knew the dangers of being identified as a translator, but he seemed to thrive on the adventure of traveling back and forth. He sometimes got a friend to drive out and pick him up at the gate. Sometimes he rode in a food truck driven by one of the subcontractors.

When it came to talking to females, Prince was endearingly clumsy. He admitted that he did not have much experience in that area. Before all of this, he said, he had talked to women in his family and not many others. He was the most religiously observant of all the translators. The second pillar of Islam calls for prayer five times a day, at specific times, facing Mecca. Prince prayed quietly in a corner of the hospital, without concern for the curiosity of the soldiers and ignoring their occasional disrespect— sometimes unintentional, sometimes not.

Prince was testing this new world and clinging to the old. He represented a new generation of Iraqis, and what a struggle he faced. He wanted it all. I asked him how he got started working as a translator, and he was evasive but said it came down to money. He dreamed about a better life for himself.

Of course, Prince did not know a life other than that under Saddam—unlike someone the age of Abu Hani, who had experienced both. Prince said he hated Saddam, but when he was frustrated that not enough in Iraq was improving he might say, "If Saddam was in power right now things would be better—less lawlessness and more electrical power."

But when I asked, "At what price?" he acknowledged the problem.

Our translators used the Internet café as we did, following the thirty-minute limit. Prince learned how to use the computer, and his world opened up greatly as he got on some of the Internet websites. He discovered a few websites and chat rooms that he probably did not need to be introduced to.

He thought most of the food at the camp was awful, and he could not understand how we could eat it. One day he said he thought America would have better food. I told him that this chow in no way resembled what I usually ate at home. He had a slender build, but he really did lose weight when he was with us because he ate carefully and generally longed for a good meal. He went home to eat good food.

We worked the night shift together, and during the last weeks I was at Abu Ghraib, we had breakfast together every morning. If I had a meeting after the shift, he waited for me. We talked about all subjects. He asked more questions than he was willing to answer, but he really wanted me to understand and hear the good about Iraq and Iraqis. He talked about government, and I always got the impression that he wanted to say more. He had more negative feelings about our government's involvement in his country. But he would always say that he thought, as individuals, Americans were great and good people.

I gave him several disposable cameras to take home and asked him to snap pictures of a day in his life—his home and where he went, friends if possible, anything. We were severely restricted by the Geneva Convention in what we were allowed to photograph. We could not take pictures of patients or of the inside of the hospital. We could not point a camera toward the prison. I eagerly awaited the photos Prince would bring to me. I wanted him to take my digital camera and camcorder, but if he got stopped with them he could get into trouble. He might have to answer questions by Iraqis who were out to get translators; Americans might think he stole them.

He took pictures in one of Baghdad's open-air markets where the local people shop: rows and rows of booksellers, people who sold artwork of all kinds, purveyors of spices, flowers, TVs, and electronics, all lining the streets. Many people congregated in the streets, mostly men dressed in slacks and plaid shirts. I was surprised by the casual, easy-going feeling in the pictures. I asked if any incidents occurred at this particular market, and Prince said most people did not fear any danger there. He got me things from the market—jewelry, ties for my husband, books, a watch, and trinkets. The quality of the items he gave me was poor. The watch worked only a few days, but I never told him.

He also brought pictures of what I think he wanted me to see, including many of his favorite statues around Baghdad. He was so sweet when he showed me the several pictures of the big Catholic church in Baghdad. He wanted me to know there was religious tolerance of Christians and that the minority Christians were protected.

He seemed to approach life a day at a time, which was not surprising given his situation. One day he wanted to stay in Iraq; the next he said he wanted to go to the United States or Australia. He asked me to help get him out of Iraq. He said he had heard that more immigrants were being easily accepted in Australia. Some days Prince dreamed of marrying an American girl who would take him to the United States. "Love would not have to have anything to do with it," he said and smiled. He was getting more comfortable in talking about his dreams, although some days he appeared to feel desperate and anxious about his future. I asked Prince if he wanted to get married someday. He said such a thing was not possible at this time.

I felt sad for him at times, maybe more so than for any of the other translators I met. He was searching and searching, and I was worried he would take too many risks and get killed. I wanted to protect him. He called me his American mother, and when he left the prison to go home, I felt like he was a vulnerable son. All I could do was hope he would be back in a few days.

We had a ritual when he came back for his night shift. I would say, "I am so happy to see you back."

He would spread his arms and say, "See, I made it back. You didn't have to worry about me."

I don't know where his loyalties were, and maybe he didn't know, either. This definitely was a new world for Prince. If he had it his way he was going to try to capitalize on what was good—he was going to go where the money was.

Mohammed

Mohammed was a handsome man with thick black hair, a great smiling face, and dark sparkling eyes. He was always dressed in jeans and a T-shirt with sandals, never anything different. He was always on the move, and he moved fast around the hospital.

Mohammed reminded me of the stereotypical car salesman. A good-natured man and a wheeler-dealer, he was on an eternal quest to make a dollar. He was the first to find out that some of the nurses loved to shop, and he was willing to bring the shopping to us.

He started with DVDs, selling us four movies on a disk for five dollars. Someone sitting in a theater must have filmed them, because we would see bobbing heads and sometimes hear incongruous laughter and talking. Sometimes the movie was so dark we could hardly tell who was on the screen. But we didn't complain because we had no alternative. I did get mad, though, after suffering through a poor-quality movie, only to have the last five minutes missing. You could tell that had happened when you heard a soldier or Marine asking, "Do you have a *Van Helsing* with the ending?"

Mohammed would always take those movies back and give us replacements, telling us he was going to have a talk with his supplier. That satisfied us, but I suspect the only talk he had was to tell the supplier to keep those movies coming. He knew even if we had a few bad DVDs, we would still buy more. Other Iraqis in the camp started selling things as well, but none were as successful at the hospital as Mohammed.

Mohammed was in his early thirties, and he smiled when he talked about being newly married. Sometimes the other translators would cover a shift for him, saying, "Mohammed is just married and is missing his wife." It seemed like he worked the least of all, but he probably got the same salary.

He was from a family of engineers, and while he had attended Baghdad University, he finished his studies at a technical school. He admitted he was the poorest student in his family, explaining with a wink and a smile that he was too distracted in college to study as he should. I believe it had something to do with women being in the vicinity.

Every one of the translators said Mohammed was the man who knew how to fix anything. They admired him for this ability. He befriended two of the sergeants at the hospital and spent time with them. I think he may have advised them on how to get certain supplies that we needed. They simply had to have a good local contact, and Mohammed always fit the bill.

Mohammed never showed fear. He never seemed to worry whether any of the detainees would recognize him, and he said he liked being a translator. Unlike Prince, Mohammed was not naïve about this new life ahead of him with Saddam out of power and a new government forming. But like Prince, he embraced anything and everything that was western. He was probably the least religious of all the translators who lived with us. He didn't say, but I believe he was a Shia Muslim. He was very casual about saying he lived in a neighborhood with Christians and went to school with Christians, talking about it as naturally as we may here in the States. He said he would not have hesitated to marry a Christian woman if the right one had been available. In his neighborhood this was an accepted practice.

He was always welcome in our common room, where we watched movies and snacked. We also used that room for weekly karaoke. I never saw him laugh so hard as when his friend Sergeant Kelly, who was a lot like Mohammed in personality, got up and sang "I Did It My Way" in his best Frank Sinatra voice.

I think even Iraqis who were as outgoing as Mohammed were amazed at how crazy and funny some of the
soldiers could be. He appreciated being a part of our private lives there. Not all of the translators got that close to
our more exclusive areas, where we relaxed and could talk
freely.

Hassan

Hassan could hardly have been less like Mohammed. He
was a young Sunni man in his twenties from Ramadi, but
he seemed a lot older and wiser than his age. He was a university graduate and had a teaching degree. While he
showed a good sense of humor and liked to talk and joke
with the soldiers, there was a very serious side to him. He
was a deep thinker.

Hassan came to work in a crisp, long-sleeved shirt and
was always impeccably groomed. I never saw him in a
T-shirt or in casual clothes after his shift was over. His
English was quite good, and he took his job seriously. He
had a lot of questions about the United States, but I never
got the impression he had any desire to visit.

He lived with his parents when I first met him, and I
know the money he earned translating was better than
what he could ever have earned as a teacher. He was helping to support his family, including siblings and parents.

He had attended an all-male college. He talked about
the fear of being forced to go into the Iraqi army, and how
men would do whatever they could to not be found and
forced to join the army.

He said Saddam's people broke down doors and
searched houses at will. One night in college he and about

eighty of his classmates were taken into custody for crimes they did not commit. Some were brought to this prison, some escaped, and the others were never seen or heard from again. He was sure some were killed and some forced into the Iraqi army, where he said men lived worse than animals. Hassan escaped and ended up in Jordan and Syria.

The day Saddam's government toppled and the day Saddam was captured were great days in his city, where, he said, the word "Saddam" could not be spoken. He was very happy that the United States was in Iraq.

Early in June 2004, he pulled me aside and said he had some good news to tell me. He was getting married in the next few weeks. He wanted to keep the news quiet and had not told some of his coworkers.

Once the decision is made to marry, weddings there happen quickly, in comparison to all the planning that goes on in the States. He said his marriage was an arranged one, as was part of the custom, but he had known the bride-to-be for a long time. "It will be good," he said. "I know you don't understand about arranged marriages, and I know you date in your country, but this is our custom and it works."

I was planning what I would do or get to show that I was happy for him. Then, a few days after he went home, we learned that his father died suddenly.

Well, that changed everything. I was surprised that he came back to work with us. We all extended our condolences. When the time felt right, I asked him if he was still going to get married. He said he could not during the mourning period. His uncle, now the head of his family, had told him that he would not be getting married in the near future. He had responsibility to his nuclear family.

He didn't say it outright, but I knew Hassan was very sad. He later told me that his bride-to-be would be told that she did not have to stay in the marriage contract and that she was free to marry another man if the family wished.

Hassan looked like his hopes and dreams were dashed. I could see it in his face in spite of his trying to laugh and talk with us. He was a well-organized young man who had mapped out his life in the midst of this chaos he was living in, and now gone was the joy and hope he had for himself. He looked burdened and lost.

He liked learning to use the Internet but was not as interested in the movies and western stuff as some of the others were. He found a special friendship with one of our female sergeants who was going through relationship issues of her own. He seemed to find comfort in talking to her, perhaps because she could most understand his sadness. He was a very respectful and kind young man.

Hassan soon announced that he was leaving the translator position. He felt he needed to be home with his family and decided to return to teaching in his city. His pay would be cut in half, but he talked about the virtues of teaching and how it was the only hope for his country—children needed to be educated if Iraq was going to succeed. That is what he had to do.

He was so sad the night before he left and near to tears when saying good-bye. I wonder about him often. Is he well in that city where there is so much turmoil? Ramadi is in the Sunni Triangle and has been the site of so much violence. Did he ever get married? Does he have hope for the future for himself or Iraq?

Kassem

Kassem and I worked the day shift initially. A shy, soft-spoken man in his late thirties, he traveled to Abu Ghraib weekly from Babylon, which was quite a distance. He often apologized for his English, but he worked hard, and as time went on his skills improved.

He worked in both the EMT and the surgical units in the hospital, and he had the strongest reactions of any translators to the procedures he had to witness. When we did painful debridements or dressing changes, he often asked if the patients could have something for pain.

I couldn't believe I had a friend from Babylon. It sounded like such an exotic and mystical place—with lush hanging gardens. I guess I didn't think anyone really lived there. Kassem said it was beautiful, with just a small military presence, "A few U.S. military patrol the area," he said. "Polish soldiers are there as well. The people of Babylon do not like the Polish because we simply cannot communicate with them at all." He added, "We like the U.S. military, and many people are able to talk with them."

When Saddam was in power, Kassem never dared to say anything about him, even to mention his name, for fear that someone might hear him and cut out his tongue or cut off his ear. He had seen that happen to others during the two months he had been forced to serve in the Iraqi army.

Kassem had worked in Lebanon as an engineer at one time. He was married while living there; he and his wife had a daughter about two years old. He was making a good living, but when the war started in Iraq he felt an obligation to return to Babylon and help support his large extended family, which included some ill members. He asked for medications such as Diovan for his sister, who had high blood pressure. He couldn't find medications in Iraq, so he got some from Jordan and other countries when he could.

Kassem did not visit with the detainees if he was not doing the official business of translating. He stayed at the back of the surgical unit rather than sitting in the nursing area as did Abu Hani, Prince, and Hassan. He feared that his family might be killed if a detainee recognized him and somehow got word to a contact on the outside.

Kassem's fear was almost realized one day. He came to work and started walking into the ward. Suddenly he was gone. I did not pay much attention at first, thinking he may have been called to another area. About an hour later the MP asked me to go to the EMT.

There I found Kassem, who was quite frantic. He had recognized a detainee who would know him, the brother of a neighbor from his home area in Babylon. Kassem was not sure if the detainee had seen him. Kassem thought that his neighbor was a good guy, but he had heard that the detainee was not. He was convinced this man could be trouble for him.

Kassem told me he was very scared, not for himself but for his family. He had put all of them in danger by doing this job. But even if he could find an engineering position, he said, he could not make much money.

Another translator covered our surgical ward that day.

Kassem stayed in a corner of the EMT, walking around only if he had to. Then he came up with a plan. Escorted by one of the MPs, he arranged to cross paths with the detainee in the walkway leading outside to the toilets, rather than in the ward. They spoke briefly, and Kassem told the detainee he was looking for a friend, as occasionally happened. Kassem offered to take a message to the detainee's brother and did so.

From that time on, Kassem was very careful. He did his job, always with his nametag covered.

Kassem was a warm and gentle person. He was respectful and shy at first and then became much more animated as we talked. He loved and adored his daughter. "In a more ideal world," he told me, "I would be thinking of more children. But not now." He was hoping to return to Lebanon someday, to find a safer place for his family.

We had wonderful conversations about our families. One day I showed him a picture of my daughter and my grandchild. He thought they were beautiful. Some weeks later, Kassem mentioned he had a nephew who painted and wondered if I would like an oil painting of that picture.

The nephew did a lovely job of capturing them on canvas, and that started a pretty good career for him, as many of the soldiers wanted the same thing done. We had little else to spend money on, and an oil portrait was well worth the price.

I sent Easter Peeps, the sugary marshmallow candy, to Babylon. They were a hit, but I was told not to send more, as the children fought over them. I sent some Milano cookies and other things for his wife, which he said she loved.

"Take a picture of us together," they said, putting their arms around each other. "Tell them that one is Sunni, one Shia, one Kurdish, and one Christian. You make too much of our differences. We can work together and get along, and we have been doing that. We just want what you have."

13

Small Pleasures and the Best Day in Iraq

There's an old saying that an army runs on its stomach, and like most clichés this one has some truth in it. Food does more than just sustain life. When it is abundant, fresh, appealing, and tasty, it serves to create happiness. When it isn't, soldiers and Marines may have low morale and unease.

When I first arrived at Abu Ghraib, our food came from the Iraq prison kitchen, and it was truly bad: overcooked, poorly seasoned, unidentifiable, and prepared with questionable sanitation. After we got the Mortar Café, the cooks still prepared beef patties, fried rice, and chicken with the life fried right out of it. But they also offered hot dogs, grilled cheese sandwiches, and, when the trucks could get through, fresh vegetables and fruit—even watermelon, once. It was a real step up from what we had been getting, and it tasted more like American food than anything we had before.

After awhile, everything started tasting the same. If they were cooking fish, the french fries and everything else also tasted like fish. When the cooks baked something sweet, there seemed to be something missing. The flour they used never tasted like what we were used to eating in the States. The pastry for pies was always bad. Cakes were lovely to look at but didn't taste good. I stopped eating those sweets.

Because we never knew what foods would be available, we became pack rats. If soda or candy bars were doled out at two per person, we took two and saved one for another day. It might be a week or more before we got the opportunity again.

Of course, we always had MREs. They came in pallets of brown pouches that provided 2,000 calories or more in each meal of entrée and dessert. Each had its own chemical heater to warm the food. We called them "Meals Refused by the Enemy," but some actually weren't too bad.

No one had control. If a truck broke down and didn't deliver what you expected or the situation was too dangerous and the trucks couldn't get through, you did without. It reminded me of being a kid on the farm in Minnesota. We didn't grow up with a lot of stuff, but we didn't complain. The soldiers didn't do a lot of complaining, either, and they were creative about solving their own problems.

I was grateful for the little things. I had Tide to wash my clothes; I had a blindfold to put over my eyes so I could sleep during the day; I had a fan set into a plastic band that fit around my neck like a dog collar and spritzed water on my face and shoulders. I had other fans to cool my skin and a neckerchief I could refrigerate and then wear to keep me cooler.

At a very low point at Abu Ghraib, my coworkers from

the pain clinic sent me a box of wonderful potpourri. It made my whole cell smell good, just about like home. Someone sent me Blistex for chapped lips and ears, and lotions, and soaps. Another friend sent me a whole box of body and bath things and home fragrance oils. It is difficult to feel feminine when you're always dirty, sweaty, and dressed like a guy, and female soldiers at Abu Ghraib really worked hard to maintain a little bit of femininity.

After I had been at Abu Ghraib about a month, I was feeling desperate to get away for a day. The Army was offering us new boots with better soles, but we had to go to Camp Victory in Baghdad to get them. I had recovered from that initial scared, wide-eyed feeling, and I deemed it worth risking the convoy for a good meal and a shopping trip. Five friends and I went to Camp Victory.

Specialist Baker would be the convoy driver. When he saw that I was going on the trip, he put his giant arms around me and hugged me. He had really blossomed at Abu Ghraib under new leadership. His job as a first sergeant's assistant gave him the independence he liked. He drove the convoy almost every day and seemed actually to enjoy the element of danger. "I'm going to give you a tour of the palace, Ma'am," he told me, his great laugh resonating well above my head.

It was a hot and sticky June day, and once again I was riding on a five-ton truck, holding my weapon out the side, ready to help defend the convoy. After getting on and off the truck many times for clearings, I was utterly exhausted. Only half-kidding, I told a young private that if we stopped one more time, I didn't think I could get back up into the truck, and he would have to push me up.

"You'll make it, Ma'am," he said.

"No, I won't. You'll have to push me up into the vehicle," I said.

"Ma'am," he said, "I can't be touching you like that."

"Specialist Evenson," I said, "I give you permission to touch any part of my body you need to touch in order to get my ass back into this truck if I can't make it on my own." He looked at me and tried to suppress a laugh, but neither of us could. It was his lucky day: I found the strength to climb in under my own steam one more time before we reached Camp Victory.

It felt like Christmas at Baghdad. We went into a huge warehouse and could take whatever we needed. I got fitted for new boots that I wished I'd had when I was in Kuwait, walking over all those sharp rocks.

I got some new under-armor bras, souped-up sports bras of heavy elastic material that made wearing the hefty vests easier. I took some wick-away T-shirts that are nice in the heat, some silk underwear, and some lightweight gloves, because the sun and heat made my weapon hot enough to burn my hands. I got some socks that were supposed to help hot, sweating feet. Our feet were swimming in sweat all day, and we all had fungal infections.

After the warehouse, we went to the Wal-Mart–sized PX and laughed and ate everything in sight. At the chow hall they even had choices of ice cream toppings.

True to his word, Specialist Baker brought us to Saddam's palace to take pictures. Then we picked up the mail and went home. For a whole day I had forgotten about everything at Abu Ghraib. It was my best day in Iraq.

Our own terrible reality crept back to us with each of

the ten miles we traveled back to the prison hospital. Outside the gate were a few dozen people, mostly women, begging for opportunities to see their loved ones—or to free them. Some days hundreds stood there, holding signs and pictures of husbands and sons. Sometimes women simply wanted to know if their loved ones were still alive.

That was only part of the pain we took onto ourselves as we entered our hell again. As we drove toward the hospital, we could see the Hard Site. The aura of what we called home was dark and eerie. *What happened here? What really happened here, during Saddam's regime?* I decided I didn't want to know as I crawled back into my cell to sleep with the ghosts of dead Iraqis. In comparison, I felt relatively safe with young, strong Marines sleeping in cells on either side of me.

Knowing that friends and family back home remembered us kept us going. The post office at Abu Ghraib was dubbed "the Pony Express." Every month to six weeks the post office would come to us in trucks and we could mail things out.

The sergeant responsible for getting out the news about mail and anything else would put a notice in the hospital hallway on a shiny white grease board. This board also carried other messages, like meeting times, special greetings, or new rules. It might say, "You will always walk with a buddy," or "Bring your gas masks starting tomorrow," or "We need six soldiers for convoy tomorrow. See First Sergeant Sullivan for details."

We were happy when we saw the message, "Post Office coming to town." Six soldiers representing the post office in Baghdad set up a mailing station, and we stood in line for up to four hours, shoving our open boxes along the floor. We had all kinds of stuff to mail home: souvenirs, books, other things people had sent us that we didn't need or couldn't carry. When the contents had been approved, we sealed them up and weighed them. Then we began to worry whether the box would make it to its destination. We wondered what we could risk losing.

Mail call was an important part of the day. The specialists and sergeants took a couple of small trucks, bigger than Humvees, to the post office and brought back boxes and boxes of mail from Camp Victory daily or as frequently as they could by convoy. On bad weeks, we might get mail only once.

There was always a great disparity of mail and gifts from home. Some had too much, while others had very little. At first I was pretty territorial with what I got, but soon I was putting things on a community table for soldiers and Marines. Ten minutes later it was all gone.

I watched to see if any of the young soldiers and Marines within our unit were not receiving any mail. Certain names were never called. I would say, "Specialist Baker, I've got a lot of food. Here, would you like some?"

"Oh, sure," he would answer, until later he started thinking I was feeling sorry for him.

Some home units seemed to forget soldiers who had been folded into another unit. That hurt the soldiers, who felt abandoned. But it works both ways. I often asked soldiers if they had let their units know where they were. And we also knew it was expensive to buy and send things.

I never felt forgotten by my unit. At Christmas in

Kuwait, Captain Betty Scott, from our home unit, got donations, did all the shopping, and sent each of us a Christmas gift of candy, socks, a picture, and a letter.

If you requested something from home, it might be a month before it arrived, and waiting for something important like a computer part was difficult. Some families worked really hard to pick the right things to send. Chocolate separates and melts. M&Ms do not melt. I got many pounds of beef jerky, breakfast bars, and drink mixes. When the fifth Harry Potter book came out, my husband stood in line with the kids to get it for me. I appreciated that.

And the transport could be rough. Some boxes reached me crushed, with tire tracks on them. I got a box with bubbles coming out of the side: a bottle of shampoo had burst. After sitting on the tarmac at 120 to 130 degrees, some boxes looked like space projects. Pressurized cans and batteries became explosive. "Hey, Larson, does your wife like you?" we asked as Larson retrieved a suspiciously oozing box.

After we had been at Abu Ghraib for a while, it didn't seem so bad anymore. We got used to the daily mortaring and our surroundings. We were surprised when someone new to the camp was aghast at our accommodations, like the soldier who told me, "You people live like animals here."

I said, "What are you talking about? It's not so bad. Look, we even have mats on our floor." He just looked at me suspiciously, with wondering eyes.

We did live like animals. Every one of us was hot and sweaty and filthy, and none of us lived like that in our civilian lives. We simply did not think about the mortar fire. It was amazing how quickly our reality changes. We kind of settle. We get our bags and our teeny square that is our own space, and we know where the shower is and know where we get our food, and the world is righted again.

Abu Ghraib had become home.

14

Challenges

These Iraqi detainee patients may not be what you would expect, and our interactions may not be what you would expect, either. This was a war experience, but a human experience as well. And as Indira Gandhi once said, "You cannot shake hands with a clenched fist."

The biggest challenge in caring for our patients was that the Iraqi detainees were on one side of the curtain dividing our hospital ward and our own soldiers were on the other. The enemy—maybe that detainee—put our men and women in the hospital. How could we set that aside and care for the enemy with the same diligence as we did our own men? And our soldiers had to accept that we must give the same level of care to the Iraqis as we give to them.

We didn't always have enough supplies for everyone. Should we exhaust our stores of blood and medications on the detainee patients, knowing that our own soldiers and Marines could be brought in at any time and need those supplies to stay alive?

* * *

I had not wanted to know anything personal about our detainee patients. It is against the Geneva Convention to ask a detainee personal questions, and a detainee might object if I asked too much. But that view changed for me early on, with a young Iraqi soldier who would not allow us to cut his hair. It was black, long and wavy, and really quite beautiful. He combed it in a western way, but he didn't want to look like a westerner. We teased him about his hair.

Through an interpreter, I told him the biblical story of Samson. I explained how Samson's hair gave him his strength and how Delilah, the Philistine woman, seduced him and betrayed his secret to his enemies. Samson was shorn, captured, blinded, and imprisoned. But after his hair grew out, when he was called to put on a show for the rulers, he stood between the pillars of the temple, pushed them apart, and brought down the temple, killing all the people who were in it, including himself.

He and the other detainees liked the story, and from then on that patient's name was Samson. He enjoyed being called Samson. He was so handsome that we told him he could have been pictured in *GQ*.

Later one day I asked him if he had a wife.

"Yes."

"Do you have children?"

"Two girls."

"Do you work?" I asked.

"Yes. I am an engineer in auto mechanics."

"Do you work every day?"

"Yes."

I was quite sure I knew the answer to this question, but I asked it anyway. "Does your wife work?"

"No."

"Do you help care for the children?"

"No. My wife takes care of the children. I play with them."

I was even more sure I knew the answer to this one, but I simply had to ask, if only to tease him. "If one needs a diaper changed, would you change it?"

Emphatically: "Never."

I told him that in the United States, men take an active part in caring for children. He said, laughing incredulously, that he would never do that. "I don't change diapers."

I said, in my best chiding, motherly tone, "You are going to go home and change diapers some day, okay?"

He knew he was good looking, and he knew we all thought he was good looking, and he was determined to hang onto his hair. Some of the soldiers and Marines thought it was sort of cool. Samson fell between conservative and fundamentalist. He would have fought to stick to some of the things he believed.

Journal entry, May 20, 2004:

I like this set of prisoners—we laugh, sing, wheelchair races. The MPs showed them the movie "Jackass!" Oh, great! Just what we want them to see—America at its dumbest. I like the MPs. I try to do any teaching I can. Am trying to do a pain management class. Help interpreters with medical words.

Most of the detainees were farmers, people from villages, and men working in Baghdad. Some had connections to the United States. One was married to an Iraqi from Detroit. She was in Iraq now, and he had never been to the States, so I think theirs was an arranged marriage. Another detainee patient had a brother who sold cars in Dallas. Others had never seen an American.

Our interpreters taught us about the differences among Iraqis from different ethnic groups or religious sects. Some of our patients were more conservative, and some, like those from urban Baghdad, were more secular. Almost everyone had dark hair and piercingly dark eyes— but we also had an albino Iraqi patient. Most of the men had mustaches; the more conservative Iraqis had full beards. The Kurdish were usually darker skinned.

In Iraqi culture, it is expected that women will wait on men and follow their orders, and some of the patients could get a little demanding. If a patient brusquely ordered a nurse to give him something to drink, a male soldier sternly told him, "Don't speak to her that way. These women are not servants. They are here to take care of you. If you can reach something, then get it yourself. Or you can drink when we pass out water or juice."

Sometimes I think they just forgot our roles, and we allowed ourselves to do the extra things they expected. Other times we had to remind them. When you see each other all day, every day, lines can blur. Then a patient might say, "Madam, I am very sorry if I offended you."

Many of the older patients spoke British English. They had studied at universities in the Middle East during a time when more English was used, and they had more exposure to the West. A couple of these were Iraqi patients identified as Al-Qaida who refused to use the translators.

According to the translators, they were Jordanian or Saudi, but they wouldn't speak Arabic because the translators would then know where they were from. The translators sometimes had difficulty understanding the southern accents of a couple of our soldiers from Mississippi, and we teased about it: "Those Al-Qaida guys speak better English than you do."

We were careful not to talk casually among ourselves within hearing of any detainee. Some had tattoos on their arms that signified they were with a certain group or gang, according to our translators. The high-value detainees had to be separated from other patients and were not allowed to speak to each other. Occasionally, a detainee would be shunned by all the others, and we never really knew why. We speculated that these were the bad guys.

One of them was my patient. He was shot to pieces, but he was going to live. He said he had been to the East Coast in the United States, but he never gave anyone any specifics. He was extremely polite. He would say, "Madam, please, if it doesn't bother you too much. I don't want to disturb you, but if you have time could you turn me now?" Or, "Madam, what time is it?" Or, "Madam, do you think I am getting better?"

My gut told me to be particularly cautious and to observe him closely. I felt he wanted to be casual and kind— break down the defenses of someone like me—so he could ask questions and get answers about what was going to happen next. I heard rumors about his identity that made me even more cautious. The CIA was very interested in him.

A ward sergeant had put a sign over his bed: "High Value Detainee." I pulled it down because a clause in the

Geneva Convention forbids making a patient's special status evident. We had to know, for ourselves, but if someone
in authority walked through, he or she would have to see
that all patients were treated the same. We followed the
guidelines, placing him closest to the MPs and farthest
from the desk. That patient was still there when I left. He
had become more and more withdrawn.

I cared for two retired generals from Saddam's army, perhaps detained because they had information gained before they retired. They were a direct contrast to each other.

The first was a retired general in his fifties who had lost
both legs above the knee in Desert Storm, the 1991 Gulf
War. His fresh injuries were minimal, and he would ordi-
narily have been cared for in the tent prison camp. However, because of his handicap, it had become too difficult
to manage even minimal cares in the tent camp. He became a patient on our ward.

This man was relaxed and rather nondemanding. His
cot was in the middle of the ward, and he seemed to command the respect of the younger men. I believe that respect came mostly from his age and his status; otherwise,
they did not seem to like him much.

The general was not well liked by the translators, either. They avoided him as much as possible. One translator said, more than once, "He is not a good man." When we
asked why, he wouldn't tell us. He would only say, "I do not
like to talk to him."

At times, the general had a good sense of humor and
looked for a laugh along with the rest of us. Yet, at other
times, he seemed to incite unrest in the ward. He spoke

out against the war and got the other patients to talk among themselves until they had to be reminded of the rules.

When I saw other patients engage in conversation with the general, it looked to me as if they spoke only out of respect for his status and were doing so very cautiously, as if they needed to be careful not to get into trouble. Yet the general with no legs continued to command an audience as he sat like a round little Buddha on his bed.

The second retired general was probably in his sixties. The story was that he and his sons owned a tire business in Baghdad where they did a fairly good trade. Iraqi soldiers had brought in all the men in his family, perhaps because one of them had gotten into something suspicious. The general had a gunshot wound to his lower back. We weren't told how he got shot, and I never learned what happened to his sons.

The general looked distinguished, and it seemed like he was accustomed to a good lifestyle—well groomed, non-callused hands, genteel manners. He seemed humiliated to be in a ward wearing paper shorts and a top. He was stoic when dressings were changed, although I knew the exit wound on his back was painful. He asked for pain medication periodically. He spent most of his time on that ward just lying on his side, not communicating with others.

When I made my patient rounds, I asked him how he was doing, and he responded in English, "Okay." I would tell him that his wound was healing, and he nodded, but he didn't respond beyond that. Sometimes he appeared to be frightened. Otherwise, he seemed distant—depressed or worried.

I suspected he spoke and understood English, but he spoke only a few words of it to me—until his last day in the hospital. He was one of eight patients being discharged back to the detainee tent camp. At that time we did not have culturally appropriate clothing available for the detainees to wear back to the camp. Often, the only clothes they had were the old, dirty garments they were captured in or the paper shorts and tops that the hospital issued. That particular day we had only a few clean cloth hospital jackets to give to the patients who were leaving—not enough for everyone.

Somehow, the young men got the clothing, and the general was going to have to go back to the camp bare chested in paper shorts. Our staff tried to find something for him but came up short. I decided to bend to his age and status.

In spite of how younger people may feel, in Arabic culture the elderly still get respect. I asked a young man who had gotten one of the nicer jackets to give it up for the general. He reluctantly gave it to me, and I handed it to the older man. One of our soldiers gave the young man a clean T-shirt from his own clothes supply.

Just before the eight detainees were removed from the ward, the general looked at me and I went over to him to say good-bye. In flawless English, he said, "Thank you, Madam, for your good care of me. I am grateful to you for that. In another time and another place, you and I could have been friends. I wish you safe travels back to your home."

He touched my hand lightly and slowly walked away with the others, escorted by an MP.

15

God and Good Old-Fashioned Fun

God works in mysterious ways, even in a place like Abu Ghraib. I never had as powerful a spiritual experience—either before or after—as I had while I was there. Maybe it was need. I knew there was little except God's grace to keep us alive.

Cheryl and I agreed early on that I would go to Protestant church services with her and she would go to Mass with me. A priest came on Fridays, if a convoy could get safely through. Soldiers, Marines, and some third-country nationals attended Mass. The third-country nationals dressed up and knelt on the cement floor. They seemed filled with faith. I often wished I could be so devout.

Every Sunday evening at 8:00, two active-duty Protestant chaplains conducted an ecumenical worship service at the Shadows. They invited everyone at Abu Ghraib who was interested in worship and praise to gather in an old meeting room, its walls painted with pictures of buildings, plants, and people indigenous to the region. The images of Saddam were covered in red paint.

Sometimes eighty to a hundred of us filed into that room wearing our uniforms, PT or camouflage, and carrying our weapons. If the lights and air conditioning were not working, it didn't matter. We held lit candles or turned on our flashlights. We could occasionally hear mortar fire outside.

The chaplain's sermons were always relevant to our situation and helped us stay on track in our lives. We praised God for our blessings. We prayed for our safety. We prayed for the safety of our families back home. No one felt excluded, whether or not they had much faith. Periodically soldiers were baptized, immersed in full uniform in an old bathtub someone found at the camp.

Soldiers from all services—Army, Navy, Air Force, Marines—made up a gospel choir. It was startling to see individuals I knew from their day-to-day work metamorphose into such experienced, talented musicians in the choir. Its leader was Tony, a black soldier who defused roadside bombs during the week and put soul into the music on Sunday. "Sing for the glory of God," Tony would say, and the singing was powerful. A couple of soldiers had guitars, and a young Marine played kettles borrowed from the kitchen. We sang both contemporary and traditional Christian songs. God, in His wisdom, brought voices together as I had never heard before.

The chaplains spent the week wandering the camp, photographing soldiers' comings and goings on foot and in helicopters and tanks. At the Sunday service, electricity permitting, they played those pictures on the screen with captions, such as, "He's flying in for the prayer service" below a helicopter landing. Those pictures were highly popular, bringing many soldiers and Marines to church for the first time and helping to keep them coming.

Sometimes the chaplains challenged us. "Bring a friend. If we get a hundred soldiers and Marines here next Sunday, I'll shave my head." We all laughed—everyone's head was pretty well shaved already.

That ecumenical service was one of the most unifying activities at the camp. Everyone—all religions—sat together, sang together, and worshiped together. I didn't see uniforms. It didn't feel like we were at the prison. I was filled with love and faith, and I could tell that others experienced similar feelings. To feel such holiness in such an unholy, dismal place was amazing. I often wondered whether that beautiful music and worship echoing through those prison halls cleansed away any of the evil spirits that seemed to lurk in the very shadows of the Shadows. God was definitely there.

In that insane place, this spiritual service kept us from getting jaded and provided balance between the soldier and the person we were—a link to home and all that was normal. We not only felt close to God there, we felt close to each other, hugging and shaking hands, filled with a wonderful feeling. I always felt like I could make it though another week after that service. Without it, I wonder whether I could have made it through at all.

I can still close my eyes and feel myself there, in that heat and dust. It became the best place in the world to feel my guardian angel and to sense the presence of God. I have searched for that same spiritual experience ever since I came home, but I have not found it.

*   *   *

Soldiers can figure out simple ways to laugh and have fun to defuse a difficult situation. Those who do it best draw on their inner child. We were fortunate to have several such individuals at Abu Ghraib.

When I first arrived we had one common area in the hospital building, about twenty by fifteen feet in size, with a table, chairs, a television, a microwave, a refrigerator, and a single computer. This was where ninety soldiers made breakfast or supper, ate, watched television or DVDs, played cards, waited for their turn at the computer, and used the computer. A counter held foods from donations and care boxes that anyone could heat and eat. Boredom was sometimes our biggest enemy. Everyone shared whatever he or she had.

We tried to get exercise because it is a good way to defuse anger and sadness, but so many roadblocks were in the way. We had freestanding weights—dumbbells. We eventually got treadmills and stationary bikes, but the electricity was down so often that they were unreliable. Some of the Marines made a little track on an old dirt road that ran around some generators, and they were allowed to run at certain times. Our unit forbade us to do that. Commanders differed on their opinions regarding safety, and this track was near the perimeter.

At first we were not supposed to provide the prisoners with any recreation. After the news of the abuse, that too changed. We began watching movies with the detainee patients. The movies could have no political references, no sexual content, and no naked women. We began with *Finding Nemo*. Later we moved on to *Trading Places* with Eddie Murphy.

A couple of our medics—nineteen- and twenty-year-olds—were comedians, drawing on their not-so-distant childhood. They organized wheelchair races in the wards and took bets on which medic would win. They had front-wheels-up races and backward races. They provided some laughter for us and for the detainees.

First Sergeant Sullivan had a karaoke machine he purchased in Germany. Newcomers were required to sing a karaoke song, and although I'm no singer, I performed "If I Had a Hammer." Some loved getting the chance to sing, some were good-natured and got booed, but those who attended had fun. There were no aspiring American Idols in our group.

Food could be a source of morale. Someone made a grill, and we had cookouts when one of the sergeants got steak or hot dogs. Families of some Mexican American soldiers sent everything for a Cinco de Mayo celebration. We wore serapes and hats, danced Mexican dances, and ate Mexican food. Asian American soldiers helped organize a campy Asian Pacific night, at which men wore grass skirts and coconut shells. It helped the unit morale to be a little nutty once in awhile.

I didn't put together parties, but my niece sent big boxes of magazines—*Smithsonian, Vogue, Vanity Fair,* and others. I made sure everyone got to see them. *Vanity Fair* and *Vogue* were surprisingly—or maybe not so surprisingly—popular with the men. They hadn't seen anyone looking like the *Vogue* girls in a while. I also shared my books.

Jeff, a medic from KBR, threw occasional parties in the contractor area of the camp. We felt honored, indeed, to receive an invitation to one of his picnics, held in the evening under camouflage netting. It was a wonderful change of scenery and cuisine—he somehow got hold of different foods.

When holidays rolled around, getting gifts from friends and family was a helpful reminder of home. They were only blips on the calendar because we didn't have the usual experience of planning for them.

By July 2004, after the U.S. military and our government decided we were going to stay at Abu Ghraib, they brought in morale, welfare, and recreation civilians who put together a small exercise area. The remodeled MWR building near the chow hall had good light, and they painted the walls white. It felt like an oasis—a place to de-compress. They had movies, exercise equipment, free soda, and television—even an off-time soldier aerobics in-structor.

Perhaps the most amazing effort at improving morale was the garden, which started as a joke: "What would you like? A garden?" Our dentist knew something about hy-draulics. His garden tools were a big green army supply chest, a hose, and a floor mat. The hose snaked up a pole and poured water onto a floor mat, with holes, suspended beneath it. When the water hit the mat it came down like a gentle waterfall into the supply chest on the ground, adding to the aesthetics of the little garden. Two live rub-ber plants bought in Baghdad sat near a children's plastic wading pool filled with water.

The temperature was 120 degrees, and I was wearing a helmet and a jacket over my army PT uniform, but it felt soothing to sit there in a canvas folding chair, listening to the sound of running water. This was also a good place to watch the sunrise. Iraq has the most beautiful sunrises and sunsets I have ever seen, with brilliant orange, peach, and golden-yellow colors that are enhanced by the desert dust particles.

But that little garden, like our shower trailer, butted up to the iso that housed the dental office used for both U.S. military and detainees. While I sat there, trying to relax and be alone for a moment, a detainee with an MP might pass by. I was in the garden but also in a fishbowl.

16

Sami and Grandpa

Longfellow once said, "If we could read the secret history of our enemies, we should find in each man's life, sorrow and suffering enough to disarm all hostilities." I thought of that on so many occasions at Abu Ghraib.

Sami was our youngest detainee, and one of the innocents. He was a muscular fifteen-year-old who definitely looked older but was truly a little boy inside. He was heavier than some of the other young guys, who were nearly emaciated. His hair was cut, while many of the others had bushy, unkempt hair. He probably came from a more well-to-do family than many of the detainees.

Sami claimed he was innocent. Unlike many others who made the same claim, he was. He had been rounded up somewhere in the Sunni Triangle as a person of interest and brought to the prison, as all detainees are. But before he was booked, the officials determined that he and some others were erroneously detained that day. After a few days, a bus came to take Sami and the others back to where they were picked up. Only a short distance from the prison, the bus hit an IED, and everyone on it was injured or killed.

Sami suffered a severe injury to one leg and had orthopedic surgery in Baghdad. An external fixator was applied to stabilize the broken bones. Then he was sent to the prison hospital at Abu Ghraib.

He came to us as a scared young boy who thought he was going home and who kept telling us he was innocent. Now he had become a victim of this war and a victim of insurgent action against the Americans. Only he was Iraqi.

Sami was placed closer to the nurses' station so we could keep an eye on him, not because of his wounds but because he was so sad and was often crying. The older detainees tried to console him, but he cried, "I just want my mother."

He didn't want to move much, and he seemed to be scared of the pain. X-rays showed that his leg was severely injured, broken in several places. We wondered among ourselves if his leg would ever heal, but age and good health were on his side.

One day when he was crying, one of our female sergeants started talking to him, and when he could not be consoled, she firmly told him to stop crying. She said, "We're trying to get you better so you can go home to your mother, but you cannot go now. You need to stay here until you can be released. I will be your mother for now, and you're going to have to listen to me if you want to get better."

He needed that firm approach, and he soon looked to her to work with him and encourage him to rehab and get better. He referred to that young sergeant as his American mother.

In the meantime, the liaison officer for the magistrate continued trying to find out where Sami came from and whom to contact to pick him up. Even with good intentions, it sometimes seemed impossible to reunite detainees with families. Most of the detainees were evasive about exactly where they lived and how to reach their families. Sami gave us the name of an uncle in a village about twenty-five miles away. We believed he did not want to give his family name, worrying that trouble could befall them.

The days went on, and each day something would occur so that he could not go. He even celebrated his sixteenth birthday with us, complete with chocolates, a care package, and a song. How to get him home? It was too dangerous for our driver to transport him. The translator wanted to accompany him, to explain what happened, but we did not want to endanger his life, as he would be unarmed.

Finally, arrangements were made for a taxi to come to the outside gate to transport him to his home. We gave him his X-rays and instructions in Arabic as to how to care for and exercise his leg. We also gave him new clothes for himself and his family, some food, cash in the equivalent of twenty-five dollars, and taxi fare to cover wherever he told the driver to go. We all said our good-byes, and he said an especially emotional farewell to his "American mother."

We never saw or heard from him again.

Almost all of the detainees in the camp were men, and I never had a female Iraqi patient. The liaison officer told me that a woman protesting at the gate of the big prison had somehow become a prisoner in the Hard Site. She was the only woman he had seen at the prison. "She was in the wrong place at the wrong time," he said.

The liaison officer, a Lebanese American, was in charge of getting the appeal papers to and from the detainees. A detainee might say, "I was just standing on the street when people started shooting, and then they shot me. I did nothing wrong." The liaison officer tried to sort out the truth of the story, and he helped the detainee fill out the paperwork for an appeal. He then delivered the papers to the military magistrate, the officer in the Judge Advocate General's Corps who decided on the appeal. The MPs were involved in this situation only if they needed to unlock the restraints so the detainee could fill out paperwork and to guard the detainee while he was unrestrained.

The liaison officer and I often met on the ward at the hospital, and we had lunch together a couple times. A compassionate man, he empathized with detainees who were caught in this paperwork shuffle. He expressed his frustration: "What is wrong with this system? It's taking *months* to get people out." He seemed to think many were innocent.

I read a news report estimating that about 85 percent of those captured are innocent, and I suspect that holds true at Abu Ghraib. The wheels of justice moved so slowly. The liaison officer was in the hospital daily trying to get appeals submitted. He made attempts to notify families, but that was a difficult task with no postal system, detainees whose families had no telephones, and detainees who were reluctant to give personal information. Slowly, innocents were being released, and with the new focus on improving the situation, coordination between the military police and others involved in the process improved.

One day I was powdering a detainee patient because he was so sweaty. He said, "That's for babies."

"Powder can be for you, too," I responded. But, as a man, he could not imagine powder being used to make him more comfortable.

I often noted that what one culture might see as normal, another sees as unusual or wrong. I certainly knew that my dress and actions were shocking to some of my patients. What's more, Americans are more apt to express themselves in body language compared to a lot of cultures. We wave our hands and give people looks. The Iraqis I met were more poker-faced. Our detainees learned how to push our buttons, especially with gender issues. One might ask me, "Do you have a husband?"

"Yes."

"How many wives does your husband have?"

When I said, "One," he would laugh. I would ask if he was married.

If he said yes, I would ask, "How many wives do you have?" Iraqis are allowed more than one wife, but most of them had only one because they could not afford another. The older general told me he had an older wife and a young wife.

The young Iraqi detainees talked very respectfully about their mothers. I was the age of their mothers, and I got more respect because of that. Sometimes that made my treatment of them a little different, too. I tried to be professional. I took more time to explain things.

teased him affectionately: "You want a U.S. woman with you at home, Grandpa?"

Grandpa entertained even the hardest of hearts there. If I saw the face of innocence while working with the detainees on the ward, I believe it would have to be Grandpa's.

A Moment in Time

Both Hashim and Sael were in their thirties, both knew a little English, and both had external fixators stabilizing badly broken legs. Sael was not, in fact, a detainee. He had been injured by another Iraqi, likely someone who had been trying to steal his car. The Americans found him and brought him to the hospital, where swift treatment saved his life. He had a brother living in Houston, Texas, so he knew something about America and the American way of life. His thinking was broader than that of many of the patients. He wore a beard and was serious but very kind in his mannerisms. Although Sael was not an official detainee, he was restrained and got the same treatment as the detainees.

We didn't know Hashim's story, except that he said he was a farmer in the Sunni Triangle area and had been captured on his farm. He said he was not involved in any fight with the U.S. soldiers. He was well groomed, looked well nourished, and was extremely handsome, with no beard. When I asked him to tell me about his family, he said he had a wife and three little children. He didn't want to tell me more, saying it made him too sad. *How could a farmer from that area learn so much English and seem so westernized?* I wondered. Somehow he had exposure to broader influences. However, between the language barrier and the fears and uncertainties related to being captured, we didn't usually get answers to all those mysteries.

Hashim and Sael came in about the same time, and both were very quiet. Their beds were across from each other at first; then they were moved next to each other. They became friends, and the two, together, became important in the daily life of the ward. They were quiet and humble, but soon the other patients looked to them as sort of a bridge between the patients and the soldiers.

We all liked them both, especially Hashim, who became a leader. We began to look to him for help with the patients. When a detainee patient who wouldn't stop crying came in, Hashim asked if he could go to the man. Although it was highly irregular, we removed Hashim's restraints and Hashim, guarded by an MP, was able to sit with the patient detainee, comfort him, and soothe his fears.

Hashim and Sael could have been Al-Qaida—we could never know, and we had to treat them as if they were, at all times. But we all felt that neither of them was an enemy. Hashim soon ranked just below the translators, as far as we were concerned. Sometimes we would have a problem or a change in routine that would be difficult to explain to a patient, such as when there was no water for showers. Hashim could explain it, and the patients were always satisfied.

Patients sometimes hoarded food, putting it between the canvas cot and the thin mattress. This caused rodent problems in the hospital, and we would periodically have an inspection of all the cots. Once again, we called upon Hashim to explain to the patients that they would be fed on a regular basis and would always get enough to eat. They did not need to hoard food. Hashim and Sael would try to make sure that rules of the ward were enforced.

We positioned Hashim's bed close to the nurses' station, and we put him in charge of the TV and VCR. He had more technical abilities than most of the other patients. He made certain that calls to prayer were always run on time.

After we had a deck built and were able to take patients outdoors, where they could get some fresh air and play dominoes, a favorite game of Iraqi men, some of the patients resisted. Maybe they were in pain or it would hurt them to move. Hashim told them, "Come now. We have a chance to go outside. Now, let's go." He set the tone, and they followed his lead.

Many of the younger patients didn't want to do painful rehab exercises. Hashim encouraged them and counted reps for them. He always led the applause when someone walked for the first time.

After having these two positive patients in our midst and having relied on their help with the others, we felt sadness upon their leaving. But it was fear that they were feeling.

We had a going-away party that evening, complete with Oreo cookies and the movie *Hot Shots*. Hashim handed me a letter, saying it was from both him and Sael. Later I asked Prince to translate for me:

In name of God most gracious and most merciful.

My greeting to all the people that I met in the prison hospital as employees such as the doctor, medics, nurses and the detainees. My Greetings are purer than rose perfume to all the people who shared with me the days of sadness and lessened the panic of the prison. Remember me when the bird warbles and when the morning sun rises. I will remember you when I see my wounds. We may not meet again but we may meet in memory. The most beautiful memories I have in prison hospital of Abu-Gharib.

I ask God for helping everyone and providing happiness for everyone (and each situation has its own speech.) Send my greetings for everyone who asks about me in Abu-Gharib.

Yours, HASHIM   Yours, SAEL

NOTICE—*Special thanks to the medical staff who worked hard to take care of me and I don't want to mention names. Special thanks to the dear brothers*

Abu Hani

Omar

Hassan

Abu Mohammed

Ameer

Ahmed

Accept my greetings.

Yours, HASHIM   Yours, SAEL

Both Hashim and Sael knew they needed to be moved to the Baghdad hospital so the fixators on their legs could be removed. But they were so frightened that neither of them slept that night. Several times, as I walked past their beds and saw them lying with eyes wide open, I told them that they should sleep. "I am afraid, Madam," they said. "I am afraid to leave this place."

The next morning, I was just finishing my shift—0615 hours. Both Sael and Hashim had their restraints off and were dressed in blue tops and disposable shorts and sandals. Sergeant Pierce and I, along with an MP, escorted them down the dark aisle and out the door to the waiting ambulance.

We had put together food bags for their trip, as we knew they could be queued up in the convoy a long time before it even began moving. Both men limped slowly and reluctantly, Sael with a crutch. They continued down the ramp, moving forward toward their uncertain future. I felt like a warden marching a death row convict to the gallows.

The scene that morning was truly memorable. The sun was just beginning to rise in the east, and a magnificent Iraqi sunrise beamed at us through the razor wire. The ambulance was backed up to the ramp. Two ambulance attendants with weapons stood on each side of the open ambulance door. The tall, uniformed MP walked authoritatively with his weapon behind the two limping, sorrowful men dressed in paper.

Hashim and Sael turned around and looked at me with fear in their eyes. "You are going to be okay," I assured them. "I know soldiers who work at Baghdad hospital. They will treat you well. You are going to get well, and you will be okay."

I then noticed that they were expected to sit in the ambulance for the eight-hour journey. That would be very bad for their legs, so I told the ambulance driver that they must lie on cots. The attendants began making the necessary adjustments.

While that was being done, Hashim and Sael continued to thank us for caring for them, and we continued to thank them for helping us with the other patients. They both had tears in their eyes, as did we.

"Don't be afraid," I said again. But the fear in their eyes tugged at my heartstrings, and I could not help myself. I put my arms around Hashim and quickly hugged him. He hugged me back. Then I hugged Sael, who also hugged me back. Sergeant Pierce did the same.

By this time the attendants were ready to put the patients in the ambulance, and the looks on their faces, as we hugged those detainees, were of pure disbelief. The MP also had a look of surprise, but nothing was said.

Sergeant Pierce and I stood side by side as both Hashim and Sael lifted their heads from their cots and waved good-bye to us. Then the doors closed on them. The ambulance drove away. The MP left.

Sergeant Pierce and I looked at each other through our tears. Our eyes asked the question of each other: *What just happened here? Who, at home, would understand that scene? Would we ever dare to tell anyone that we hugged prisoners?*

After much thought, I maintained that I was still a good soldier. I realized that the military can make a good soldier out of a mother but it can't take the good mother out of the soldier. It was a moment in time for me, in this crazy, mixed-up place, when I looked at those men not as enemies but as two men needing human expressions of understanding. They were not just pictures in a magazine of people on the other side of the world suffering. They were standing in front of me. Maybe I wanted to put my arms around all the innocent suffering people in Iraq at that moment.

I will never, ever, forget that moment of my life.

Anything But R & R

I called home and talked to Dave as often as possible. Our conversations were pretty unemotional and general in nature because we had no privacy. Dave was concerned for my safety and needed to hear my voice often for assurance that I was still okay. But like many spouses, he didn't want to know too many details of my life at Abu Ghraib, and I did not tell him how bad things were there.

It seemed he was also trying to protect me from being concerned about him. Shortly after Memorial Day, Laura told me that he had injured his arm in an accident and hadn't been able to go to work.

I called Dave and asked him about it. "Did you go to the doctor?" I asked.

"No, I've been taking ibuprofen and putting ice on it."

Less than a week later when I was talking to our friend Carol, she mentioned the surgery that Dave would be having. "Surgery?" I asked.

"Oh," she said. "Maybe I shouldn't have said anything. I assumed you knew."

I called Dave again, and he still downplayed it. "I'll be okay. Don't worry about me."

But I did worry about him. I knew it would be fairly serious surgery with a long rehab. Maybe his condition was worse than he was letting on. Obviously he didn't want me to be concerned about him, but I wanted to be there. I needed to make sure he was okay. I asked my commander for a leave, since I had now been on active duty for fifteen months with no end in sight.

Commander Gilles tried to convince me to hang in there and wait until the end of my deployment. "No," I said. "I need to go home. I didn't take leave when I was in Kuwait because I thought I would be going home soon. My husband is having surgery, and I want to be there. I promise I will come back in ten days and finish my commitment here. I will willingly do my duty for as long as I am needed here. But I need to go home now."

Commander Gilles helped arrange R & R for me. I would arrive home on June 14, the day of Dave's surgery. I would have to return to Abu Ghraib, though, and stay on with Commander Gilles and twenty others, the last of our unit to leave. When I told Dave, he said he didn't want me to come—it would be too hard for both of us to have me go back to Iraq. I knew that what he was saying made sense, but I couldn't stay away. I had to be sure he was okay. I had to go home.

The translators got an inkling that I was leaving and were not happy about it. I promised I would see them again, but Abu Hani didn't believe me. The translators said the detainees liked me best, and I decided that was a compliment.

*   *   *

I left on a convoy Friday morning, June 11, and arrived at Baghdad International Airport to bad news. "You're not going anywhere," I was told abruptly. They had some questions about my leave orders. This is the difficult situation when attached to another unit. We fall under the medical brigade in Baghdad because we are in Iraq, but the real line of command still exists in Kuwait.

After several hours, the ticketing agent reluctantly let me go with some civilian contractors and try to work it out in Kuwait. I turned over my vest and weapon to my sergeant driver and said good-bye.

At Camp Wolf in Kuwait they were nicer about it, but they said the same thing, "You're not going anywhere." After six hours, they finally found my name under Coalition Forces Land Component Command. I was in the last R & R group processed out of Camp Wolf, my first and best home in the Middle East, which was closed a few days later. I was sad to know that I would never see it again.

I called home and told Dave, "I think I may get home for a few days. I'll know when I see you." I couldn't give him specific information for security reasons.

The process for getting out of country is long and involved. I had to go through a Post-Deployment Health Assessment and answer questions about my physical and mental health. Next, I went into an amnesty booth with a drop box, where I could get rid of any prohibited items: ammunition and grenades, weapons, gifts made of special kinds of wood, pornographic movies or books. No one could say they were not given a chance to freely give up something that was prohibited.

The next step was customs. This was always a frustrating process. I worked so hard to stuff my duffle bag, sitting or jumping on it, just to get everything into it. Then I dragged it through the line until it was my turn, and all that I had so laboriously packed was emptied onto the table and checked by the soldiers running the customs areas.

At this point, I was so close to getting my ticket punched to get out of the country that I wanted nothing to go wrong. If I was pulled out of the line, I might miss my chance of leaving. If they found anything illegal, disciplinary action would follow, and I would not get home.

When I was finally cleared, I quickly repacked everything. I was in luck. With the help of a strong, friendly soldier who pulled the flaps together, I could get the lock on. By now, hours had passed, and I started to wonder if Dave was right after all. *Was it worth all this to go home for ten days?*

Finally, the bags were taken and we waited for the bus ride to the airport. At last we boarded a regular U.S. carrier, with flight attendants and everything. I left Kuwait at 0130 June 14, long after I expected to be home.

I arrived in Minneapolis at 1130. Dave had just returned home after his surgery and was still recovering from the effects of the anesthesia. I was so happy to see him again. We both cried. At that moment, I realized how much I had missed him, and I was so glad to be home.

Laura cried when she saw me, and that made me cry as well. I think all that stuffed-in emotion was just breaking out and allowing me to feel again. I knew how much she had been helping her dad, and I kept thanking her and apologizing for not being there. She kept saying, "I'm so glad you're home" and "It's so good to see you again."

Both Dave and I slept most of those first two days. I hadn't realized how exhausted I was. Then everything became uncomfortable. I didn't know my own house anymore. I didn't know where things were kept. As wonderful as I felt seeing my family again, it proved to be a terrible time for me. Dave had been right. I felt as if I had been drop-kicked into the real world for ten days, but it didn't belong to me yet. I couldn't claim it.

Laura spent little time with me the first couple of days, to give Dave and me time together. Even later, she didn't know whether she should be there. I felt disconnected from everyone and everything. I couldn't allow myself to feel like I was home because I couldn't stay.

Dave and I talked a little about our plans for things we would do when I came home for good. The future was uncertain for Dave, as we didn't know how much use of his arm he would recover. Our plans for buying a lake home—our dream—became tentative, but I told him to keep looking.

The temperatures were a little cooler than usual for June in Minnesota, and I was cold most of the time I was home. I mostly wore sweatshirts. The last couple of days we had some pleasant walks around our neighborhood. I told Dave more about my friends in Iraq.

Laura had arranged for me to get a haircut and have a massage, manicure, and pedicure. It all felt wonderful. I renewed my driver's license and my nursing license. I was overwhelmed by choices. I ate ribs at Famous Dave's and a Peanut Buster Parfait at the Dairy Queen. The world looked colorful.

YaYa, my granddaughter, looked at me but went to Dave. Laura felt bad about that, but I told her I understood it would probably happen. I was glad to see she was close to Dave. During the last couple of days, however, I got her to warm up. I needed to make sure she knew me.

I spoke with many friends and got to see everyone I needed to see. One day my parents and sisters and their families and Dave's family came for a get-together. I felt so odd. Like I hardly knew any of them. Like I didn't want to feel close to any of them. My time there was so temporary.

Everyone asked the same questions. "How are you? How can you stand it there? What's it like? How do the Iraqis feel about us? Are we accomplishing anything?" Over and over I heard those same questions. I talked about the good things soldiers were doing, human kindnesses, and Iraqi translators.

I kept thinking, *I got to see the people who are important to me. If I die, I will at least have seen them once more.* I was not being fatalistic—just realistic.

One day I went shopping for things I wanted to bring back to friends in Iraq. The day before my flight back I got all my packing done. I wanted to just get back to Iraq and get it over with so I could come home and be me again.

Because Dave couldn't drive yet, my son-in-law drove Dave and me to the airport. Dressed in my desert uniform, I sat in the back with my granddaughter. I was grateful we couldn't loiter. I got out quickly, grabbed my bags, said a hasty good-bye, and walked through the airport doors. I didn't look back. I was a soldier again. I was keeping my end of the bargain; soon I would come back home for good.

Both Dave and Laura told me later that they thought I cared more about my soldier friends in Iraq than I did about them. They thought I looked so eager to leave again. They didn't know what a facade that was. They didn't know how empty my heart felt. I could not bear to get too close when I couldn't stay.

19

Back Home at Abu Ghraib

The trip back was uneventful. I was now a seasoned traveler in such uncomfortable circumstances. I was happy to see my cell was still waiting for me, just as I had left it. Nothing was yours at Abu Ghraib; anything could have happened while I was gone. A few soldiers and Marines had gone home for good, and a few soldiers and Marines were on leave, but otherwise not much had changed, except that I was put on night shift.

After being gone for a while, I could see that many active-duty soldiers were given leave after having been there a few months. And although everyone denied that Reservists faced discrimination, Reservists were not given the same consideration. It was harder for our unit's command to advocate for us. We were detached, split up, and under the command of the medical brigade in Baghdad, but our true command, the one that took care of our personal issues, was back in Kuwait. This made me think hard about our unit and my role as a Reservist. Many of us were mid-career professionals. In civilian life, members of our group worked at some of the best medical facilities in the world: the Mayo Clinic in Rochester, Minnesota; Rush Hospital in Chicago; and Cleveland Clinic in Ohio. Our operating room nurse celebrated her sixty-sixth birthday while in theater. We brought a wealth of knowledge and life experience to the mission. This became glaringly important at Abu Ghraib, where we augmented a young staff, bringing a consistent, fine balance of expertise and maturity.

Of course, because Reservists tend to be a bit older, they have more medical problems, including hypertension, thyroid issues, and the effects of a long history of smoking and the use of various medications. The environment in the Middle East is unforgiving, and a soldier who is not in good health may suffer from serious problems. Dehydration when taking certain prescribed medications, for example, can endanger your life. Chest pain was one of the most common nonsurgical problems we evacuated out.

We had seventeen active-duty soldiers folded into our mission in Kuwait; when members of my Reserve unit were sent to Iraq, we augmented units of active-duty soldiers. Active duty and Reservists worked together, and I think many attitudes changed as we recognized each other's strengths. We are still not one army, but this Middle East experience is moving us there.

I am proud to say that I have stayed around long enough to have worked with and blended in with all the different military services in their work for Operation Iraqi Freedom. I have nothing but respect for the sister services. We worked intimately and well together.

While we worked together well as individuals, Reservists had less voice to take care of their own as a group. Our units were broken up and reassigned to others, squandering the bonds of trust, dedication, and fairness we built as we trained together. We had fewer privileges and fewer opportunities for leaves or four-day trips out of theater to decompress. Lengthy deployments were causing irreparable financial and marital problems for some Reservists. In general, we were heard less. We sometimes had to fight hard to take care of our soldiers.

Yet the Reservists and National Guard soldiers were playing a vital role in this war. The mission could not continue without the ongoing involvement of citizen soldiers in medical units, hospitals, and every other area and specialty.

The Nameless and Faceless

I knew the soldiers in my unit in Kuwait so well that I could identify any of them by name just by the way they walked, talked, or wore their uniforms. But at Abu Ghraib, we were faceless and nameless and we all looked the same. I might be telling a story and try to remember someone; all I could remember was that he had short hair and was dressed in beige. That was about as distinctly as we looked at each other at times. We could usually tell the person's gender, but with all the gear we wore, even that was often impossible.

We all wore desert beige uniforms. The Army, Navy, Air Force, and Coast Guard had a large beige and brown print. The Marines wore a beige pixel print uniform that easily separated them from the rest of us.

A Kevlar helmet generally obscures a person's looks, but you can quickly learn a lot about someone walking toward you. We scanned each other to look for rank, branch of service, and shoulder patches indicating organization and unit. Recognizing rank was especially important if you were in a salute area where you were required to follow this protocol for military courtesy.

The military police were the most easily identifiable at a distance. Their uniforms were the same as everyone else's in the Army, but they wore a light brown leather armband with the bold letters MP stamped on it.

About a dozen military police, three of them women, rotated into the Abu Ghraib hospital while I was there. Several were in police work or studying law enforcement in their civilian life. I suspect their units assigned them to the hospital position because of their personalities.

Some of the MPs liked the assignment, and some did not. If they were not working in the hospital, they would be working in the in-processing area, where the new detainees were brought into the prison. The temperature was hot and tempers were emotionally charged there. They would act as security guards and assist with moving detainees from one area to another. We heard that in-processing was a tough area, a far cry from the hospital.

The hospital had air conditioning, yet it wasn't always fun and games. The MPs said medical staff and nurses "babied" the detainees. Some of them simply couldn't handle that. When an MP released a detainee's restraints for a bloody and painful procedure, the MP had to guard closely, looking tough when he felt like throwing up. Some of them had never been in a hospital setting and had not been prepared for this aspect of their duty. They also had to take the detainees to the porta potties, where they sometimes ended up having more hands-on duty than they bargained for.

Some of the MPs wanted to learn why we dressed a stump of a leg in a certain way, why a patient had a colostomy, and why we put a wet or dry dressing on to debride a wound. Others didn't care and preferred to work a station at the door of the hospital unit instead of on the ward floor, so they could guard the ward as a whole and watch a movie on their computer. Overall, they were a fun-loving group who found hospital workers to be an unusual collection of soldiers. As medical personnel we are often perceived to be good listeners, and we found that some MPs started hanging around with us more and more on their off hours.

A lot of those MPs were more compassionate than they would like us to believe, and I had a hard time thinking that any MP I worked with could have abused prisoners. They were asked to help us stay safe and keep order in our hospital wards, and they did that. I think they previously thought our hospital jobs were easy, but they found out otherwise. Just as we may say to them, "How can you do the job you do?" they say the same to us. I believe we earned each other's respect.

We were all just surviving. And as closely as we worked with each other, we rarely discussed our civilian lives. We all just wanted to do our job, stay alive, and go home. That day couldn't come fast enough for any of us.

Many civilians played a huge part in our daily life at Abu Ghraib. The U.S. government contracts with civilians and businesses for a great many military needs and to support rebuilding. In Iraq, many of the contractors hire people from third countries, such as India, Sri Lanka, Pakistan, and the Philippines.

I heard stories about how people were hired. Some families in these countries were very poor. A contractor's agent might offer a father what seemed to be a lot of money for his son to work in Iraq for a year, promising him a good job. Then the workers are taken far away to work in military camps. They may be hired by one contractor, then subcontracted to another.

They are paid poorly by our standards, do not get any perks, and work very long hours at manual labor. Workers in our camp were cleaning, cooking, and feeding thousands of soldiers and Marines. Many told me they wanted to go back home but could not earn enough money to do so.

They lived in small trailers close to the kitchen with little personal protection against bullets or mortars. We could see clothes hanging on lines strung from their trailers. Some of them sat outside their trailers and smoked, never leaving their tiny area. It seemed they had nothing to do when they were not working.

Some of the third-country nationals had never been anywhere else in their lives. Many were curious about American soldiers. They would stare at us, but they were evidently told never to talk to us.

One of the men laughed and joked with us when we went through the chow line. He wanted a pair of sunglasses, so I found a pair for him. When I went through the line to give them to him, he wasn't there. "Where is that guy who wanted the sunglasses?" I asked. The others shrugged. They didn't know. They weren't supposed to talk to us. I never saw him again.

Some civilians came as volunteers. Lance, a retired civilian bus driver from the United States, was an older man who looked like he could have been a Wal-Mart greeter. He came to Abu Ghraib to make the soldiers' lives a little easier. He started a shuttle service from the hospital to the chow hall to our respective living quarters. We appreciated not having to walk across that hot, dusty, dangerous area.

When the government was turned over to the Iraqis in June 2004, I commented to the translators about what a success, what a wonderful step forward that was. They just shrugged their shoulders and indicated it meant nothing to them, it wouldn't help them. I was glad to know, months later, that it did make a difference to them—and to the millions who voted.

I sometimes talked politics with our translators. They were more interested in our choices for U.S. president during that election year than they were in their own politics. They also told me they liked Americans as individuals but they did not trust our government. I asked what they wanted me to tell the people back home.

"Tell them not to leave us like the last Bush did. We suffered greatly because of that."

They also told me, "You should have less military presence here, and have less involvement in things our people can handle ourselves. Managing the traffic flow in Baghdad, for instance," they said. "If you would let us do it we would not have the problems because we know how to handle our drivers."

Sisterhood

Americans often think that Muslim women cover themselves because men make them. I learned, however, that the reverse is true. "We want to be covered," an Iraqi woman told me. "When we get married it is only for our man to look at us. For us to save ourselves for him. The girls here wear short skirts. In your home you can be dressed like that for your husband. I am dressed for him. I don't want others to look at me. It is my husband I want to look at me."

I was once riding the hospital elevator in Kuwait, wearing my uniform, when a local woman got on with me. She wore an *abaya,* a veil that covered her completely. As soon as the door closed, she said, "Hello."

I said, "Hello," smiling. She suddenly opened her black gown and removed the cloth from her face. She was dressed right out of Saks Fifth Avenue. She smiled broadly, looking like she nearly wanted to hug me. "See, I'm just like you," her eyes said.

Obviously she had money. She was dressed to the

nines. When that elevator door opened again only a few seconds later, she walked out modestly, totally covered again. But we had communicated, woman to woman. It made my day.

On another elevator in Kuwait, I was riding with two male soldiers when five women and two girls got on. They tried not to look at the men, and they all started giggling. Because I was in there, squished in back with the men, it was safe to get on the elevator. They were still giggling when they got off.

There was always that testing—that curiosity about us. That's why I always wanted to represent both the U.S. military and America with dignity. You never knew who you were going to encounter.

At the chow hall I met a female translator, Ablat, who worked in a different area of the camp. She was a Shiite from Basra and had three sons, one of whom was a medical student. Saddam had killed her husband in 2000. She was very angry about that. She worked for the Coalition Provisional Authority as a secretary, and she loved Americans. She wrote love poems and songs and sang a Lebanese song to me one evening when we had dinner together. We laughed a lot. She loved to hear about similarities between American and Iraqi women.

She told me that some translators tried to exploit detainees for money. She left suddenly, in fear for her safety because she had turned one in for dishonesty, and I was told she would not be coming back. I was sorry I never had the opportunity to read her poetry.

*   *   *

Once the KBR laundry service was established and became more reliable at Abu Ghraib, we had a laundry lady who lived in Baghdad and worked at the prison. Her name was Shaqria. She traveled back and forth by convoy at least five days a week, putting herself in great danger for this job.

Everyone at camp welcomed this laundry service when it started. They set up a metal structure the size of a semi-truck trailer. Fluorescent lights hung in the dark structure with rows of shelves on either side. A wooden counter across the front served as the official check-in and pick-up spot. We put our laundry in blue mesh bags and filled out a slip of paper indicating how many T-shirts, pairs of socks, or other pieces of clothing we were turning in. Sometimes the wind was so strong that we used the rocks kept on the counter to hold our papers while we fought to hold onto our clothes.

When the day was exceptionally hot, they hung camouflage netting over the counter to offer a little protection from the sun. Usually the lines were not too long, unless a group of soldiers was returning to camp after having been out for many days.

I met Shaqria at that counter. I was wearing all my gear and struggling with both my clothes and the laundry list in the hot fierce wind. She came over to assist me, looked me straight in the eye, and smiled. From that day forward, we became friends to the degree we were able.

Shaqria was in her late thirties. She spoke only a little English, and I spoke only a little Arabic. But after a while it didn't seem to stop us from communicating. Her husband did not have a job, so he stayed home with their four children while she worked. It was clear that Shaqria and her husband must have had a desperate financial situation, as it is an embarrassment for an Iraqi woman to work outside her home, and especially to work for an American company. And Iraqi men are not usually caretakers of their children.

Shaqria brought a picture of her husband and children for me to see, and I showed her pictures of my family. I gave her shampoo and some great-smelling Victoria's Secret perfume, and she gave me a painting of the Iraqi countryside. I always tried to bring my clothes to the counter at midday on my day off so we could talk. One day Shaqria told me that she took my clothes to her home and washed them herself to make certain I would get them back. I was really touched by her kindness.

We were curious about each other and tried to answer each other's questions. I told her about my job at home. She said she was a Muslim, but she wore brightly colored shirts and a skirt and was never covered like most Muslim women. She said she did not cover herself at home, either.

I asked, "Are you not afraid to come to this prison every day?" She said she must, as her husband did not work. And that was that. She did not talk about fear or the need to work. She just did what she had to do.

I never saw her around the camp or eating at the chow hall. I only saw her behind that counter or coming out to help me at the sorting table. When it was time for me to leave, I wasn't allowed to tell her I was leaving, but she guessed as much. I brought her and her coworker, another woman with whom I had become acquainted, some bath and body products. She asked if I was leaving.

I said, "Yes."

"Go home to your husband and be happy," she told me. "Don't forget me. Call me every day." Then she gave me her cell phone number.

On my last day there I saw her and she began to cry. So did I. Her boss knew we were friends, and he let her off for a half hour so we could just sit together. She said, "We are friends, right?" I told her I would never forget her and the picture I had of her would always remind me of her big smile and her warm heart.

I think there is a bond between women, race or culture notwithstanding. There is a sisterhood. Sometimes at Abu Ghraib I wanted to go out to that prison gate and say to the women standing there, "We are taking good care of your husbands. They are safe. I want to assure you that they are not being mistreated." I'd like to think it would have given them at least a small measure of comfort. Maybe I would have felt better, too.

Finding Myself Again

Leaving Iraq was happy; it was sad; it was as surreal as arriving there.

Some of the translators handed me letters.

From Abu Hani:
When I came to Abu-Krab to work for TITAN *I thought I was going to see some things and I did. I saw dignity, loylity, happeness, cleaverness all in one person that all in* GERMAIN.

From Prince:
To my second dear mother.
These words I am writing for you represent my respect, esteem and my love for you. All what I write can't represent all what I have for you. Generally I can say you are my second mother so when I see my mother I remember you. I promise that I will never forget you till death and I hope that you will never forget me. Separation always separation is what I dislike in life but at

this moment I have duality in feeling because I am sad because you are leaving for ever leaving me alone. Second I am happy because you will go home to meet your family. My last words: enjoy life, take care of yourself. At last you are my real friend.

From Breeze:

Dear Germain,

It's been so nice working with you although it was for short time but I acquired useful medical terms. Thanks for being so nice to me and to all the translators. They always complimenting you for being kind and nice. I am unhappy at your departure. I hope you come back to your home safely.

It was hard to say good-bye.

The hot, dusty, dangerous convoy, the waiting, the delayed and confusing flights to Kuwait, the waiting, the turning in of gear, the waiting—all familiar, all disorienting. We spent four days back at Fort Stewart, attending sessions about going home that were to prepare us to meet our spouses again, to get back into the civilian world again, and to face the difficulties of regaining our normal lives.

At our first formation back at Fort Stewart, we were told we should wear our green uniforms. I didn't want to. *No. I've been over there. I earned this dirty desert uniform.* I could feel myself seething inside whenever I was expected to wear the green. The desert uniform represents the real deal, the experience a veteran of that war has that separates him or her from soldiers not deployed. It represented where we had been and who we had become. To give up the desert uniform says you have assimilated to being back. I was not there yet.

I returned home on August 21, 2004, with no fanfare. We were just a few. Being in the safety of my husband's arms once again was so wonderful. I was grateful to see Laura, YaYa, and my son-in-law again, knowing I would be able to see them every week and watch YaYa grow up. Yet I soon felt as if I were floating between two worlds.

I thought that I knew what the adjustment would be like and that I had some control over the process. But I had thoughts, feelings, and inner chatter that could not be rationally controlled. My mind was in Iraq, but my body was here, where it quickly felt like it didn't belong.

Meanwhile, no one in the United States seemed to care that we were fighting a war. The conversations around me were on such insignificant matters—day-to-day concerns, the state fair, what to buy for fall, anything but the war. I didn't think it would be like this. I couldn't *stop* caring. In every quiet moment my mind was back at Abu Ghraib with patients, fellow soldiers, and translators. Were they safe? Were they okay? I was listening to any news I could get about the war and the Middle East. The newspaper reports said too little, and television news was not much better. Sometimes I found myself yelling at the TV, "That's a damn lie. It's just not true!"

CBS began devoting a minute every evening to a soldier who had been killed; I stopped whatever I was doing when I heard the lead-in music and was glued to the television set. I prayed that I would not recognize that day's soldier.

As I watched the segments, I couldn't cry. I hadn't cried since I returned home. But I said a prayer for that family.

Amazingly, I felt unsafe in my safe, quiet suburb. I didn't have my weapon, I didn't have my gear, and no one was guarding the bridges when we drove. At first, I was unable to sleep unless there was noise of some kind, and I frequently jumped up at night looking for my weapon. I was not a combat soldier, but even as a nurse I was trained by members of the infantry division at Fort Stewart, learning how to defend a convoy, rescue fellow soldiers, use my weapon, use a gas mask, and many other soldier skills. I used that training, day in and day out, in Iraq. When it was time to go home, I was expected to drop it all and immediately go back to my former life. It was too much.

Dave and I functioned like business partners as we reviewed finances, retirement savings plans, and bills. I tried to listen and be part of conversations—to be "normal"—but most conversations were of no interest to me. I had to walk away. I didn't feel normal.

My family and friends tried to help me acclimate myself to being home again. Their love, support, and understanding sustained me from the moment I got word that I was activated, through the entire time I was away, until I got home. However, they didn't know whether to be gentle or to ask the questions they wanted to ask. I knew everyone was walking on eggshells around me. I knew I created that environment. But I didn't know what to do differently.

Eighteen months of change had occurred at home while I was in the Middle East, and I was expected to catch up immediately. The Reserve unit I had been part of for ten years was deactivated a week or two after I got back. My granddaughter, who was only ten months old when I left, was two and a half years old when I returned. When my family greeted me at the airport, she looked at me and asked, "Who are you? Where did you come from?" I could see how close she was to Dave, yet she didn't even know me. It broke my heart to see what I had missed.

I went grocery shopping at my local Cub Foods store. A clerk whom I knew well said, "Gee, I haven't seen you around for a while."

What could I say? "Oh, I've been in Kuwait and Iraq for eighteen months"? I didn't want to tell people that—my emotions were still too raw. I just smiled and said, "How are you?"

When people asked me what it was like, I simply said, "It was a hard life, and I am happy to be home." I could not explain eighteen months of my life in a few words.

I was so exhausted. Getting up was not a problem, but getting motivated to accomplish tasks was. Making simple decisions was difficult. I didn't much care about my own health. I was so used to thinking *today could be the day I get killed* that it didn't seem very important. I never felt sorry for myself. I just felt such sadness—I had a heavy heart.

My husband and my employer both felt I should decide for myself when I felt capable of going back to work. I had some fears about it. I had started my job at the pain clinic only four months before I was called to active duty, so I was just getting into the swing of it when I left. What would be the expectations? Every week I said to myself, "I think this is the week to decide." That week came and went, and I promised myself the same thing the next week.

There is a fine balance between giving oneself enough time and lingering too long over a decision. Finally, Mo, a good friend who owns my favorite coffee shop, said, "Bring in your calendar next Wednesday, and we'll sit down and set a time for you to go back to work." That was the best thing he could have done. I needed that extra kick—something I would never had needed as my old self.

E-mails from friends who had also returned home from the war confirmed that they, too, felt as if their world was spinning differently. While we were all happy to be home, none of us had a smooth transition. We could always rely on our battle buddies for understanding.

I called Cheryl frequently, and those were some of the few times when I could genuinely laugh. "My husband threatened to send me back to Iraq only twice this week," she told me. "It's getting better!"

Almost a year after I returned home, I attended a social gathering of soldiers from the 114th, my home unit. We chatted with friends, celebrated retirement, and reminisced about our military life together. Then I noticed Major Trent Stanley standing at the bar alone. He had been in Iraq before I got there and had served in Baghdad before coming back home recently.

When I greeted him, I felt like I was looking into a mirror. *He's not home yet*, I told myself.

He said he was happy to be here, but he didn't look happy. He had a distant look and a bit of sadness about him. I recognized that numb stage—that floating feeling, not wanting to connect with anyone or anything. He used to have a wonderful loud laugh. Not now. Like me, he could not reach out to anyone.

"I know what you're feeling," I told him.

We talked about the footlockers we had sent home. I had immediately opened mine, sorted things, separated my green and desert clothing, and then never opened it again. He hadn't been able to open his yet.

Major Stanley, a combat stress nurse in the Army and a mental health nurse at a va hospital, deals professionally with post-traumatic stress disorder in patients. Like many of the returning soldiers, he wants to be part of this world, but at the same time he fights it. He used the analogy of a dvd playing a movie in his head: "You can work at turning it off or just keep it running." Those who can't learn to turn it off continue to suffer.

All the dreaming and planning Dave and I did in those months apart came true for us. We bought a lake cabin in northern Minnesota, and I found a kind of peace in spending summer weekends there. We moved from being business partners to being husband and wife again. I was finally able to start turning off my movie. The balance was shifting, and my thoughts about things at home were greater than those about my other life.

I officially retired from the military on September 1, 2005. The former me would have stayed with the Army and worked toward a promotion and a new job. I loved my army life, and I miss my military family—but I love my family more. I hope to return to Kuwait and Iraq again someday in peaceful times.

I am different now. I love being a nurse practitioner, but my job isn't my life as it was before. I used to be a social person. Now I am so private. I have a short fuse. I am not on a single committee, at work or otherwise, and I don't want to be. I am able to say "no." In a way I feel as if this is my chance to rewrite my life.

Sometimes I feel sad for soldiers. It's not a new sentiment, but that doesn't make it a less valid or heartfelt one. No one who hasn't done the job can realize how tough it is and the private sadness and loneliness we feel. We are torn between our families and our duty to country. We only hope that our families will understand and be waiting there for us when we get home. But family relationships can be stretched too far, especially for the young men and women who leave their small children for a year or more. A chaplain once told me that those marriages that are strong would stand the test of time while those that are fragile would be severely tested.

I guess I was one of the lucky ones.

Epilogue

The medical units who staffed the hospital at Abu Ghraib after we left continued the record of excellent care for detainees. Colonel Leslie Rice, chief nurse of the 344th Task Force, reported this exchange with a patient in 2005:

> *When we were finished, I asked him, via a translator, if he had any questions. He spoke for a few seconds and then covered his heart with his right hand, which is a sign of respect and gratefulness. Through the translator, he said he wanted me to know that throughout Iraq, our hospital and staff were known as angels of mercy. This statement was unprovoked—and surprising.*

On September 2, 2006, Abu Ghraib was formally handed over to the government of Iraq.

Four people whom I will never forget touched my life while I was in Iraq. They died making a difference.

Angel, our ambulance driver, was shot in the head and died in southern Iraq in 2003. He was at a rally point bringing patients from Iraq to Kuwait. It was a dangerous mission, and after his death ambulances no longer were used along that route.

Our young postal worker, Frances, who was always laughing, handled many of my packages. Her job was hot and difficult. She worked at Camp Wolf in 2003 and then transferred to Iraq. She was in a helicopter going home on leave when it crashed and killed her.

One of my cellblock Marines, a man whose name I never knew, died when his tank caught fire during a fight just outside our gate at Abu Ghraib. His own ammo heated up and exploded as he tried to get free. Three others in the tank were injured but survived.

Our partner and KBR paramedic, Jeff, designed that little clinic, and he always took special care of his contractor patients. He was a hard worker who could make things happen, like those picnics he coordinated, and he supported us as military. After I left Iraq, he was killed by small arms fire when he stepped outside his clinic one day.

*   *   *

The mortar fire blasts loudly, and I awaken with a start and reach for my weapon. Then I realize it is only the crack and rumble of a Minnesota thunderstorm. I lie back down in bed, bring the blankets back over me, and fight with the movie in my head to be still and quiet. I keep worrying about the people I met and thinking of the difficulties my family endured. I feel a profound sadness that will not let me close my eyes.

But the wind and booming thunder that once would have frightened me now soothe me. As I listen to the storm outside and the storm in my head, I begin the routine to release my horrors by counting my blessings. I am home with my family. They are safe, and I am safe. I then recall the face of every person I met on my journey to hell and back, each person whom I will never forget. I thank God that I met them, and I ask for their safety. As I reach the end of my long list, rain falls softly on the roof, thunder rumbles in the distance, and the movie's volume diminishes.

After a while the movie is dark and silent. Sleep can come again.

Acknowledgments

This account of my service at Abu Ghraib reflects my own experiences and memories, which will no doubt differ from those of others who were there. I have changed the names of the people with whom I served to protect their privacy; I have changed the names of the Iraqis I met to protect their lives.

This story has become a book because of the talents, perseverance, and enthusiasm of Connie Lounsbury. She showed great sensitivity when I initially hesitated to return to my memories of Abu Ghraib; she persisted patiently, through hours of interviews on Monday after Monday at her beautiful country home, always keeping me on track; she asked probing questions and provided insightful organization. I owe her a special debt of thanks and gratitude.

I am grateful to the good friends and neighbors who supported my family when I was gone. They eased the burden for us.

I thank my husband, Dave, for his willing to support so

many of my dreams—in education, in military sevice, and in this book project. He has always believed I could do it, even when I had doubts.

Connie and I both want to express our deepest gratitude to Ann Regan, editor in chief at Borealis Books. She has worked tirelessly to make us look good. We also extend our appreciation to other press staff members for their good work.

I would like to thank my many military friends and colleagues for their support and encouragement while this book was being written, including Specialist Gray of the 67th CSH from Würzberg, Germany, who sent me some of the photographs. A special thank you to Lieutenant Colonel Cheryl Proper, my battle buddy.

Finally, many thanks to Atik, Eduardo, Pradeep, Rose, Dolly, and Beena, my dear friends from Kuwait, who taught me so well what true friendship is all about.

I am donating my royalties from the sales of this book to the Fisher House Foundation, which helps to support soldiers and their families. It is worthy of your support, as well.